Marr
to tl
MINISTRY

Sarah Meyrick grew up in the Cotswolds. After a
degree in Classics at Cambridge, she worked in
publishing before becoming a journalist. She is
now Chief Reporter at the *Church Times*. She met
her husband Ben, who is a vicar, at university. They
live with their son and daughter in a pub-turned-
vicarage in Oxfordshire.

Married
to the
MINISTRY

SARAH MEYRICK

To Martin
with best wishes

Sarah Meyrick

TRIANGLE

First published in Great Britain in 1998
Triangle
SPCK
Holy Trinity Church
Marylebone Road
London NW1 4DU

British Library Cataloguing-in-Publication Data
A catalogue record for this book is available from
the British Library

ISBN 0–281–05007–4

Typeset by Pioneer Associates Ltd, Perthshire
Printed in Great Britain by
Caledonian International Ltd

CONTENTS

—⁓⁓⁓⁓⁓⁓⁓⁓—

*For Ben, who has never asked me to be
anything other than myself*

Bishop: Will you strive to fashion your own life and that
of your household according to the way of Christ?

Answer: By the help of God, I will.

The ordination of priests, *Alternative Service Book*, 1980

FOREWORD

~~~~~~~●~~~~~~~

The sphere of a clergyman's wife is, of course, a more subordinate one than that of any other wife. It calls for an absolute surrender of self. Her first object must be to make the surroundings of her husband's life such that he can do his work easily; to make no claims upon him which would interfere with or hinder his work. Any help she can give him should be known only to themselves and God. At the outset she is called to make a renunciation of that complete sympathy and confidence which is the ideal of a loving wife ... I need not say there must not be the least suspicion of jealousy.

Those words were written by Louise Creighton, whose husband was Bishop of London exactly 100 years ago, and the echo of such highmindedness still lingers. Small wonder that one of my two childhood resolutions was never to marry a clergyman (the other was never to marry a man with a beard). Later, I justified my evident lack of principle on the grounds that I wasn't marrying the sort of cleric I'd sworn not to marry, ie I wasn't about to become a vicar's wife (it was harder to explain the beard). And then we moved to a parish, and I discovered – like thousands before me – that the vicar's wife is in some ways the very antithesis of a stereotype: the parish priest still has privileged access to all sorts and conditions of people, and this is often extended to his wife. Perhaps there should be a bumper sticker: 'Vicars' wives reach the parts other people's wives cannot reach . . .'.

Nowadays, as Sarah Meyrick makes clear, it's quite likely to be the vicar's husband discovering that the privileges of being a clergy spouse impose their own pressures: tied accommodation, to take but one example, is both a blessing and a curse which clergy families have (depending upon your point of view) enjoyed or struggled with for centuries. We may no longer be subject to quite the same burden of expectation as our predecessors, but there are fresh challenges: it is actually increasingly difficult, in a society that emphasizes the rights of the individual, to admit to the vicarious stresses or vicarious fulfilment of a role that is dependent upon – and a direct consequence of – your relationship with someone else.

This challenge (like tied accommodation) is not, of course, exclusive to those who are married to the ministry. Perhaps the unique pressure on clergy spouses is that we are often guilty of stereotyping ourselves: we may find it difficult to complain when we feel we should be counting our blessings – even though the two need not be mutually exclusive. Smoking with repressed anger can certainly damage your health and negative navel-gazing doesn't get us anywhere. On the self-help principle it's good to know that you're not alone and to be able to draw on the experience of your fellows. Sarah Meyrick's new study is not only good-humoured, well written and thoroughly researched, but has the singular advantage of being written from the inside: she understands the pressures on the clergy spouse because she is one – but she doesn't look like a vicar's wife, and that, of course, is a compliment.

Caroline Chartres

INTRODUCTION

'Some very sensible women I know will repudiate this book at sight. They are, in fact, married to clergymen, but they strongly object to being treated in any way as special cases. I heartily respect their point of view, and must say at the outset how unattractive is the picture of parsons' wives chewing self-centredly over their own exclusive problems. Why must we separate ourselves from other women, turn the spotlight on ourselves, and make such a fuss?' So wrote Ceridwen Higginson in 1967 in the opening chapter of *Such As We Are: A book about the parson's wife, by parsons' wives*, echoing the ambivalence I feel beginning this book a generation later.

There are any number of reasons a book on clergy spouses should not *need* writing; and yet, overall, I think it does. Many clergy spouses today would identify with the objection to being 'special cases'. Why should we (and I have a vested interest in this, being one such spouse) be treated as a separate category, different from anyone else? In the ideal world, the very notion of the 'clergy spouse' would cease to exist, beyond being a rather quaint way of referring to someone who happens to be married to a priest. To talk about 'clergy wives' is to come up against all the stereotypes so many contemporary partners of clergy are, in my experience, so keen to

1

shed. Of course we are all different, we are all individuals in our own right. To try and make generalizations about the thousands of diverse women (and some men) who happen to be married to the thousands of equally diverse clergy is like trying to pick up a hedgehog: the subject resists the very attempt, and you begin to wonder why you tried.

I doubt that anyone today would consider writing a book about the spouses of teachers or plumbers or doctors. In contrast, there have been any number of books and articles on clergy wives in recent years. Whether we like it or not, the subject is alive and kicking, and interest extends well beyond Church circles. Joanna Trollope's *The Rector's Wife* was highly popular both as a novel and a TV drama; Susan Howatch's Starbridge blockbusters are bestsellers. In March 1996, the *Sunday Telegraph* published an article entitled 'Clergymen's wives have their own cross to bear' alongside 'A week in the life of a vicar's best helpmate'. In the summer of that year, both *The Sunday Times* and the *Church Times* added a new twist with, respectively, their articles 'The Vicar's Husband' and 'Clergy families – when do *we* get a look in?', each written by a male spouse and thereby opening up a new perspective on old ground.

Is there anything new to be said? What – if anything – makes us so worthy of discussion, so 'special', particularly when our greatest hope is that we will be seen to be 'normal'? During the course of my research for this book, I met with a whole range of reactions and responses. 'Not again,' said one woman, who contributed a chapter to a book about clergy wives in 1983. 'It didn't do much good last time.' Another wrote, 'What makes a clergy wife any different from any other wife? Isn't part of marriage to learn how to deal with each other's jobs and to compromise? We're no different from any other professional couple.' A third said, 'While the divorce rate among clergy is so high, there is something important to be found out.' Another, 'I congratulate you on the research you are doing and hope that the results when published will spark some improvements in the care of clergy and their families.'

In 1967, Ceridwen Higginson concluded that the subject needed to be addressed because there was 'real evidence of unrest, uncertainty, and distress among these women, evidence which is startling in view of the special access to joy and peace which they might be supposed to enjoy'. But the main reason, she continued in her introduction to *Such As We Are*, was her conviction 'that the whole regrettable self-consciousness, the distress, the fuss, the strenuous repudiation of fuss, are symptoms of a truly unprecedented situation.'

There are five particular reasons for my thinking that there is cause to address the subject of clergy spouses again, now. First, I think there are certain oddities ('our own exclusive problems') about the life of the clergy, which are especially acute in the parish setting, that result in specific tensions between work and family life. Second, I am intrigued by the fact that stereotypes about both the clergy and their wives – and I mean wives – have proved so enduring. However inaccurate, dated or laughable, these remain the backdrop to the debate. I did wonder if perhaps I should call this book 'Such As We Aren't', as many of us appear to have a stronger idea of what we are *not* than of anything else, even if the general public hasn't quite caught on yet. One minister's wife expressed this ambivalence well when I asked her if she had an image of a 'typical' vicar's wife. 'I don't know, but I know I'm not her,' she replied, 'but I can't imagine myself being anything else.'

Third, I am interested to see how far the huge social changes that Britain has experienced in the last 30 years or so have changed the perception of the clergy and their families, in the eyes of the public and in their own. Fourth, the advent of women priests (and therefore

3

priests with husbands), combined with other recent changes in thinking within the Church about ministry, has inevitably had an impact on the sorts of expectations imposed on all clergy and their households. Finally, I have myself seen real evidence of distress in many (but by no means all) of the people I have come across in the course of my research.

WHAT'S SO SPECIAL ABOUT A CLERGY MARRIAGE?

I remember going to have my hair cut on the morning after Princess Diana's famous *Panorama* interview. No one in the streets or on the bus could talk about anything else, and everyone had their own opinion, something I commented on to the hairdresser. 'Yes,' she said, and laughed. 'I suppose it's a bit like that, being you?' I agreed that if you overlooked the small matters of the bank balance, jewellery, and full complement of staff, it had its similarities. There are, of course, many jobs that entail a degree of public exposure, long and/or antisocial hours, being 'on call', working from home and regular relocation.

In their book *Holy Matrimony? An exploration of marriage and ministry*, Mary Kirk and Tom Leary asked the question, 'What makes clergy marriages distinct?' They quote one bishop who told them, 'There are differences with other marriages and also similarities. It is the total package that makes clergy marriage a special case.' He went on to list the factors that, when combined, he thought marked out clergy marriage. These were: tied housing and fixed-term appointments; few resources; moral standards; a public image to keep up; expectations to be an ideal family; the ill-defined boundaries between work and home life; doing the Lord's work, so that spouses compete with God; and coyness about using counselling agencies when difficulties occur. To these, Kirk and Leary add their own list of contributing factors,

4

which include a high incidence of illness and depression; a high incidence of problems relating to sex and gender; the perception of work, necessarily done in other people's leisure time as 'not a proper job', and social marginalization and isolation.

They go on to say, 'The clergy wife and family wrestle with the fact that their position gives them a good house, a recognized social position, job security, a husband/ father who is seen more frequently than most but who, at the same time, is less available, *and* that money is a problem, *and* that they may have few friends living nearby.' Such paradoxes, they argue, lead to a degree of confusion, and may (but not inevitably) lead to difficulties: 'Areas where such confusion and, therefore, potential conflict can occur include the home, the family, money, confidentiality and boundaries.'

'Boundaries' was one of the recurrent themes in conversation with the clergy spouses in my research. What sort of boundaries – if any – do clergy and their families attempt to set up between work and non-work, time off and availability, privacy and hospitality, parishioners and friends, and how realistic or desirable are these? Janet Finch, in *Married to the Job?*, in which she looks at what she calls the 'incorporation' of wives into their husband's jobs, concludes that the most significant factors leading to a wife's incorporation within (and eliciting her contribution to) her husband's work are any job entailing flexible work hours; working from home; living in an institutional setting; work that is 'socially contaminating' (in other words, which results in a wife being recognized as the 'wife of . . .' even in a purely social sphere); and any kind of self-employment. Geographical mobility, tied accommodation, and the husband's job involving a certain amount of 'women's work' also contribute. In these terms, the score of the parish priest shoots off the scale.

Interestingly, she also notes: 'The case of the clergy of the Church of England provides an example – albeit quite a rare one perhaps – where a worker is formally *expected* to replicate work relationships in the home, since he is specifically required to promise to do this at the time of ordination.' Hand in hand with this requirement goes the public expectation which demands different moral standards of the clergy than of the rest of humanity, and seizes on any perceived lapse with alacrity.

So, even if a spouse chooses not to become actively involved in their partner's ministry, it is virtually impossible to avoid becoming a part of it, at some level. This is perhaps most graphically illustrated by the domestic aspect of life in a clergy house, whereby work comes into the home. One woman described this particularly well in *Married to the Church?*, a book a number of clergy wives each contributed a chapter to: 'How can I begin to describe the frustrations of the life and the job – not my job as a French teacher, but the job that's inevitably thrust upon me simply because I'm married to a clergyman. Do I really want to answer yet one more telephone call, when I know that all I'll have to say is "He's out, will you ring back again later?" Can I bear to have our evening meal interrupted by a telephone call for the thousandth time? They know that we're always there between 6.15 and 7.00 so that's when they ring. I feel like screaming, and quite often do . . .'

Whether or not being a clergy spouse is perceived as a burden or a joy will, of course, vary from person to person, and no doubt from parish to parish, or even from day to day. During the course of my research, it quickly became apparent that different people were happy or unhappy about diverse aspects of their partner's job: to one, the shortage of money was a pressing problem and a cause of great misery; to another the difficulty was having time off together; a third was thrilled by the welcome she and her children had met with in her husband's parish; another professed to be living in one of the best houses in the country. Most of those I surveyed

6

had some positive things to say about their partner's ministry, and their place within it, yet the vast majority had also at one time or another struggled considerably with some aspect of it. Barely anyone felt there was nothing to discuss. As one friend who contributed some of her own battles to this book said, 'There's no doubt about it. It's a *very* weird job.'

THE ENDURING STEREOTYPE

In 1982, Rosalind Runcie, the wife of the former Archbishop of Canterbury, wrote an article in *The Times*, 'Clergy wives are people too'. It began, 'There is not a typical wife of a doctor, lawyer, or dentist, so why should there be a depressing and unflattering Identikit image of a clergy wife? Usually this is of a drab and uninteresting human being, ground into submission by her husband's job, running all the parish groups and generally being a do-gooder. It is high time that someone tried to show that this image is out of date. Reveal that you are married to a clergyman, when meeting strangers, and you would be surprised at the reaction. People ... can be astonishingly rude. Sometimes they are patronizing and tell you that you don't look like a clergy wife. What is the answer to that back-handed compliment?'

What has changed, I wonder, since 1982? Why do people still say, 'I'd never have known you were a vicar's wife'? 'I've heard that at least fifty thousand times,' one woman told me. Another said, 'People say I don't look like a clergy wife. Does that mean she should still have tweeds, brogues and grey hair in a bun? Why on earth is presentation so important to people?'

Does anyone ever say 'I'd never have known you were a vicar's husband'? Somehow it's hard to imagine this being said without conscious irony. Personally, I would much prefer not to be termed 'a clergy wife' at all, not only because I find it peculiar to be categorized by my husband's job, but also because it suggests that I am married to the clergy in general, rather than to one man who happens to be a vicar. (I would feel just the same about being called an 'army wife' if I were married to a soldier or a 'school wife' if I were married to a teacher.) I react more strongly still to being referred to as part of a 'clergy couple'. There are many genuine 'clergy couples', where both partners are ordained (although they might equally prefer not to be categorized purely in terms of their jobs), but this is not so in our case. However, for the purposes of this book, and to avoid the unnecessarily long circumlocution 'person married to a priest', I have given in to using the shorthand 'clergy wife', 'clergy spouse' and 'clergy family'. (The fact that 'clergy wife' appears more often is, of course, down to history.)

The vicar's wife of George Eliot, Anthony Trollope, Jane Austen or Barbara Pym, doing good in the parish and serving her husband's needs, lingers on in the public imagination. Everyone, it seems, can conjure up a picture of the 'traditional' vicar's wife. Somehow the stereotype endures, even where it is acknowledged to be out of date; it remains the point from which we so often begin, if only to try and shed it as quickly as possible. This is well illustrated by an article that appeared in *The Independent* in 1993, which opened: '[She] is 56, an attractive, dark-haired, intelligent woman. She is married to the vicar of [L], but doesn't look it, which is a slur for a start. How should vicar's wives look? Well, she appears dynamic, a no-nonsense sort of woman who would look good in big shoulders, directing some thrusting campaign. She's done a bit of that, despite her life as a vicar's wife and raising three children.' The subject of the article was a woman who had come to terms with a particularly unusual upbringing; in later life she was at various times a Labour councillor and a magistrate, and currently holds a full-time post in education. Yet, from the outset, the journalist chose to define her in terms that were entirely incidental to the body of the story.

Nearly every single one of the women I contacted for this book had their own idea of what a 'typical' vicar's wife was like; none would admit to being her. One woman wrote, 'Though the clichéd description of a vicar's wife as an "unpaid curate" is perhaps an overstatement, I see the role that tradition has defined for her as primarily that of helpmate to her husband in many of his parochial tasks. The fact that most priests still work out of their homes and that the vicarage often serves as a meeting place for parish groups means that clergy wives are inescapably drawn into the supportive work of answering telephones and doorbells, taking messages, conveying information, lending a sympathetic ear, providing hospitality, and helping to manage their husbands' schedules. Beyond the assistance she provides on the domestic front, the vicar's wife, who is typically a regular church-goer, is usually involved in one or more parish groups or activities – a contribution that is still, I believe, expected in most congregations. My perception is that the average clergy wife, whether by design or default, devotes a considerable share of her time and energy to serving her husband's parish.'

Nearly everyone claimed to know someone who matched up to their image of a 'typical' vicar's wife; a few felt such figures existed only in the imagination, or were no more than ghosts from the past. Here are some of the descriptions I heard: 'a good organizer'; 'worthy'; 'terribly Christian'; 'dowdy'; 'providing support for all areas of her husband's ministry'; 'she knows everyone'; 'a hostess, secretary and shoulder to cry on'; 'a listener'; 'a bridge-builder and fence-mender'; 'a home-maker'; 'the proverbial "good wife"'; 'an example to other women in the parish'; 'always welcoming'; 'boring'; 'in orbit around her husband the vicar'; 'teaches Sunday school'; 'visible at every church function'; 'uninteresting'; 'self-sacrificial'; 'someone who bakes cakes and makes biscuits for church meetings, supports her husband and does not think about her own needs'. One woman concluded, 'Above all, she is capable. I think tradition has a lot to answer for. So does my predecessor.'

SOCIAL CHANGE

A book about clergy wives published in 1991 talked of the increasing number of clergymen 'letting' their wives work. Very few couples today, I suspect, would think in these terms. For anyone who grew up during or after the 1960s and 1970s, the weight of 'traditional' expectations can be at worst oppressive and at best bewildering. For my husband and me, in our early thirties, the idea that our working patterns should be anything other than a matter of joint discussion and decision or that the upbringing of our children might be less than a fully shared enterprise or that the domestic burden should not be shared is quite foreign, in a way that would not have been the case for a previous generation.

The last few decades have seen significant changes in the structure of family life. Couples in the 1990s face changing patterns of work, mobility, financial insecurity and often juggle two jobs with the demands of bringing up a family. There is the added dimension that, as Christians, we may have a different agenda. However far we conform to the pattern of the world, or not, there is no denying that, in the space of a generation, the goal-posts have moved. Our Christian response to prevailing social conditions – issues to do with family life, work, our material needs, questions of gender and sexuality, ideas about community – is reflected in the choices we make.

One of the key issues within the Church at the moment is the future role of the clergy. In the Anglican Church at least, financial worries, the ordination of women to the priesthood, the shortage of ordained clergy, together with changes within society, have led to a dramatic reshaping of ministry.

Both clergy and lay people are being forced, however reluctantly, towards a major, and sometimes painful, rethink about the sort of ministry that is practical and desirable as we move into the next millennium. For all the development in lay ministry, non-stipendiary (NSM) and local non-stipendiary ministry (LNSM), old inherited concepts about 'the parish priest' are often ingrained. Transition from one pattern of ministry to another may be greeted with enthusiasm or resistance, but almost certainly with a degree of confusion and ambivalence. Where do such changes leave the clergy, and their families?

For some rural, multibeneficed clergy this will mean the unbearable pressure of being forever spread too thinly over too wide an area, villages finding it hard to let go of the idea of having 'their' parish priest who is always at hand. NSMs, meanwhile, have the problem of devising their own working patterns and availability, as they may also have a full-time paid job. Women priests, though welcomed with open arms in some instances, still battle with hostility and a lack of acceptance elsewhere. And, of course, how the clergy – and the people among whom they work – feel about their ministry inevitably has an impact on the rest of the household.

However, debate within the Church in recent years about matters of gender, sexuality, equality and oppression, together with the decision to ordain women as priests, means that many of the old attitudes towards the role of women and men are being rethought. Could the ordination of women to the priesthood result in the great

11

liberation of clergy wives? For some, perhaps, it might be seen as a threat as they may fear that somehow their position might be usurped. For others, the fact that the number of clergy husbands (of whom nothing or little is expected, it appears) has increased, is a huge relief, and the deathblow to old ingrained attitudes.

EVIDENCE OF DISTRESS

The first Christmas after my husband was ordained, a family member asked me how things were going. At the time, I was pretty miserable: we had moved to a new area, miles from any of our friends, into a house I disliked, I had left my job behind, and our first child (a dreadful baby) was born within six weeks of Ben's ordination. Becoming 'the curate's wife' was the final straw. Altogether I felt diminished, which I tried to express. I was told in no uncertain terms that I was making a fuss. My husband's ministry came first: I should give more to my marriage.

The idea that if we express less than exhilaration with our lives as clergy spouses we are 'making a fuss' (Ceridwen Higginson's 'whole regrettable self-consciousness, the distress, the fuss, the strenuous repudiation of fuss') is a pervasive one, overladen no doubt by the moral code that most of us as Christians attempt to follow. Somehow we fear that feeling angry or unhappy might be our fault. In *Married to the Church?*, one wife opened her contribution with these words: 'There have been many times when I wished I was not married to a priest; I have never wished I was not married to Anthony. I feel the need to begin like this, because what follows may well seem disloyal. Some people may feel that any criticism of a clergy marriage must undermine the work of the clergyman in question. Some may think me selfish; others may say that the problems of being married to a priest are no different from those of any marriage.' She went on to describe her own experiences as a clergy wife, and how she and her husband attempted to resolve some of the difficulties they encountered.

The 1996 *Sunday Telegraph* article 'Clergymen's wives have their own cross to bear' opened: 'The wives of Britain's clergy are miserable. Their men are never at home, because they are too busy listening to other people indulging the modern craze for talking about themselves', and continued with accounts of intense pressure, loneliness and general misery within clergy marriages. At least one of the women who was quoted subsequently objected to the piece: she claimed she had been misrepresented. No doubt there were specific reasons for her annoyance, but I can't help feeling that she, like many of us, really did not want to appear to be 'making a fuss'.

Here are two illustrations of real evidence of distress from my own research. One comes from a clergy wife whose husband had left a prestigious career in the armed forces and was ordained after 11 years of marriage: 'I hate it! I wish he'd never got ordained,' she says. 'If I'd known at the time he first thought about it what it would have entailed, I would have given him an ultimatum – the Church or me.'

Another, an American, wrote to me from the USA, where her English husband is now a minister: 'In answering the questionnaire, I was astonished to discover how angry I still am at much of what I experienced as a clergy wife in England. Having had an entirely different, and vastly better, experience of the role in the Episcopal Church (ECUSA), I now know that being a clergy wife need not be the ordeal it often is within the Church of England ... I find it inconceivable that the English Church does so little to support clergy families and that it continues to embrace structures that are

13

unquestionably hard on them. The issue of clergy care, which is very much to the fore in ECUSA, seems scarcely to have been addressed in the C of E.'

I would not want the tone of this book to be unduly negative. Rather, it is an attempt to look at some of the ways in which the clergy and their families are, at this particular time, tackling some of the tensions that, although not unique, are specific to their job – how they integrate a vocation (or vocations) with work, home and family life – overall, the sorts of choices they are making. Some spouses were clearly unhappy with their lot, and, indeed, I came across a significant number of people for whom the floodgates opened when I raised the subject. A sizeable number, though positive overall, and excited about their partner's ministry and their own role, also expressed a great sense of relief in being able to speak out honestly about some of their struggles.

WHO I SPOKE TO

This book has inevitably grown out of my own experience. I wrote it in part because I was taken aback to discover quite how completely our own lives – and the percep-tions others had of us – were overturned when my own husband was ordained. We married while he was still at theological college, and I thought that I had some idea of what I was letting myself in for. I was quite wrong.

The difficulty in writing this sort of book is, of course, to achieve any sort of picture that is accurate or useful beyond the personal; in short, to be representative. For every reader who agrees with what they read, there will no doubt be others who will say, 'It's not like that'. Such a book could never be exhaustive, and mine certainly does not claim to be. However, in order to spread the net as widely as possible, I carried out interviews with 50 clergy spouses, either face-to-face, by telephone or by post, or by a combination of all three. I tried as far as I could to include the experiences of families from north, south, rich, poor, urban, suburban and rural areas across the country, and from a range of churchmanship.

The spouses of those I interviewed were predominantly Anglican, coming from the Church of England, Church of Scotland and Church in Wales, although I also included a number of Methodist representatives, to see how far there were areas of overlap and difference. As it is still early days since the priesthood of women in the Church of England, and male clergy far outweigh the female clergy in number, my survey focused more on households where the clergy are male, although I do discuss the experience of clergy husbands in more detail in Chapter 8. As the vast majority of those who generously shared their experiences with me preferred to remain anonymous, all names have been changed.

1

IDENTITY AND
EXPECTATIONS

I was pushing the pram down the street of the market town where my husband had just become curate. Although exhausted from night-feeding, I was feeling an element of satisfaction in the fact that the baby and I had managed to leave the house in a moderately presentable condition, neither of us bearing any obvious sign of stale milk or sick. Above all, my two-week-old son was, finally, asleep, allowing me a brief stretch of mental freedom. Two women approached me. 'We want to see the curate's baby,' said the first, elbowing me out of the way. I stood back, a little surprised, as she peered into the pram. 'Hmm,' she said to her friend, doubtfully. 'Pity he's not more like his Dad, isn't it?' She looked at me accusingly. 'I suppose he's warm enough?' 'Funny name for a parson to choose, don't you think?' said the friend. 'Oh well,' sighed the first. 'At least he's got a son. That's something.' Without another glance in my direction, they turned and went, leaving me utterly defeated.

IDENTITY

This incident brought home to me two uncomfortable facts. First, that, as a family, we had somehow become public property. Second, that, whether or not I saw myself as having any sort of 'role' in the parish (and I didn't), the public nature of my husband's job conferred a vicarious identity on me, even if, as in this particular case, I was to all intents and purposes invisible.

In *Married to the Job?*, Janet Finch argued that 'being a public figure essentially means being defined in terms of work for the purposes of almost all social contacts. Such situations seem to be produced by a combination of characteristics of the work itself and the setting in which it takes place.' The wives of such men, she continued, experienced a vicarious 'contamination'. 'This means that they experience some of the consequences of being a public figure without having been appointed, elected, or paid to be one. Nevertheless, in certain circumstances a wife will be expected to behave *as if* she had been.' We have all witnessed this in the run-up to political elections in the USA and the UK; the politician's partner is packaged and presented to order, an integral part of the whole vote-winning process. On a much smaller scale, this is echoed in the experience of many clergy spouses.

The degree of public exposure of a minister, and therefore his or her family, varies from job to job. In spite of the commonly held view that the clergy are increasingly perceived as marginal to mainstream life, many of those I interviewed felt that their partner had a public role within the community, and that this was something that at some level touched their own lives. This is far more the case in a parish setting (rather than a sector ministry), and more commonplace in rural areas. While for some people this visibility opens doors, and provides an easy way in to the heart of a community, for others it can be a source of irritation and resentment.

'For better or worse, we are a well-known family,' says Becky, who is married to a suburban vicar. 'Keith gets asked to do things in the community. It extends to me in so much as mothers at school feel free to talk to me

17

about personal things because they feel "safe" with me. It's fine, absolutely; and much easier after a few years just to be yourself.'

Alice, whose husband is a college chaplain, says, 'I was invited to become part of a group, including a health visitor and college tutors, who set up a course for mothers to talk about their feelings, and stresses and so on. I was no more qualified than many other mums, but I was considered already to have a public role. I think it is important to be part of the community you live in, and not to set yourself apart. It's something I'm happy with.'

Others find it more oppressive. One wife, Caroline, says, 'I remember when Benedict had only been ordained for about a year, and we were still struggling to adjust to everything. When we were on holiday, we went to the local church, and the members of the congregation were very friendly and welcoming after the service. I suddenly realized that they were talking to me – I mean *me* – not as an adjunct of him, or because they wanted me to give him a message; for the first time in a year, I was suddenly being treated as an individual in my own right.'

'If anyone at church ever introduces me to a newcomer, they say "This is Melanie, she's our vicar's wife", as if I'm some kind of symbol,' another woman told me. 'I find it irritating sometimes as I'm never just "me" – I'm a figure of whatever that person's imagination and background makes me.'

'I think it's quite difficult to be an individual in your own right,' says Jo. 'Certainly in our last parish I was very much "the wife". On interview I was shown where the local supermarket was – that being my main interest of course! I was rarely called by name. Even in the school where I worked I was introduced to the other staff (some 100 plus) as "the new curate's wife". I was incensed, as it labelled me for my entire two years there. I once attended a pastoral workers course in another city and I deliberately hid the fact I was a clergy wife; they didn't find out for about 18 months and it was wonderful.'

This discomfort with the label was reflected in the many comments I heard on the efforts some people make, in certain contexts, to conceal their 'identity'. 'When I meet people in the community, I do try to hide the fact that I'm the vicar's wife for as long as possible,' says Julie. 'I prefer that people can get to know me for who I am before writing me off with all the false preconceptions that they might have.'

'We never tell anyone we meet on holiday what his job is,' says Charlotte. 'I'm proud of Mark's ministry, and fully support everything he does, but it's so nice when people treat you as an ordinary family for once.'

One of the oddities I have been aware of at times is the sharply contrasting effect the clergy identity has on churchgoers and non-churchgoers. Within the Church, the clergy are frequently treated with a certain deference and, at times, inappropriate elevation, resulting in the 'what a privilege to be married to such a holy man' sort of comment, which always leaves me grinding my teeth. Outside the Church, you meet embarrassment ('Excuse my language, vicar') and even mockery, which can be equally painful. One of the least enjoyable evenings we have spent since Ben's ordination was at a dinner party, where our host, a vague acquaintance from his school-days, spent the first hour of the evening taking bets from the other guests on what my husband's hilarious profession might be. We did not return the invitation.

A number of others felt that this superimposed identity actually hampered their own Christian ministry. 'I am a deeply committed Christian, and as such I have a job to get close to people who are not, and to share the love of Christ,' Katie told me. 'My being a vicar's wife restricts me somewhat because people expect me to be ultra-spiritual. I can get closer to non-Christians when they don't know who I am. I'm always shocked at what a non-Christian thinks a vicar's wife should be like. They expect plums in the mouth, the hair-do, twinset and pearls and all that sort of thing. All the older vicars' wives I've met are like that, I'm afraid. When people discover I'm the "vicar's wife" they're shocked rigid – and sometimes angry, as if I should have told them first.'

'One of the difficulties I have found is in leadership,' says Jo. 'I am increasingly taking on roles as a "leader" in the parish, and we have even discussed my doing lay reader training. David himself says that if I wasn't his wife, he would have approached me by now on the subject. But because being a clergy wife is a role in itself it is quite difficult to assume any other kind of leadership. For example, David is going on a course soon, and he would like me to lead the family service while he's away – because I lead a home group, run the music group and work with children, *not* because I am the vicar's wife! But we feel people will think I'm doing it because I'm the vicar's wife. I would like to be *me*, a member of the congregation, with particular gifts and training that can be used, not "Mrs J the Vicar's wife".'

A JOINT MINISTRY

In *Married to the Church?* Myrtle Baughen, the wife of the former Bishop of Chester, describes her experience as a vicar's wife about 30 years ago: 'I remember arriving in our new parish with our children – a 5-year-old daughter just starting school, 19-month and 5-month baby sons – and being asked to give an hour's Bible Study to the ladies' meeting. I tried hard for the first two weeks, but had not managed to prepare for the third week. So Michael suggested I led a discussion. It was disastrous . . . but they were sweetly understanding, and soon we worked out a pattern that was right for me, and for them and the parish.'

Few clergy spouses today would be likely to find themselves in Mrs Baughen's impossible situation, although she is in no sense protesting ('for me,' she writes elsewhere, 'the joys of being a clergy wife so outmatch the frustrations'). But times have changed; today many clergy spouses have careers of their own, and for others, their interests and skills lie outside the sphere of their partner's job.

The 'unpaid curate' has surely long disappeared. Of the spouses I interviewed, only about half said that they were 'actively involved' in their partner's ministry, although the majority said that they provided background help, from answering the telephone to offering hospitality. As the vast proportion of clergy spouses are themselves Christians, they are likely to value their partner's ministry highly and to be supportive, if only emotionally. Many said they regularly discussed ideas with their partners; another said she was 'an ear' at church, 'to pick up what he might have missed'; a third said she was 'the person he discusses things with and off-loads concerns to'. Others had more active roles in prayer groups, children's work, music, helping to lead services or even preaching. Only a few said they were not involved at all: 'I keep out of it,' said one husband, 'it's her job, not mine'; 'I'm not often here, as I work miles away,' said another; 'I try to go to church sometimes,' said a wife.

'Involvement' comes in many shapes and sizes. 'I'm personally very supportive – we share everything,' says Becky. 'I am very involved with toddler things because of my own child. I'm completely happy about it, especially as I end up with masses of people in the house, all linked with the church, but they come as friends. My involvement has been getting to know people, *not* running groups, and after five years here I think the majority of people accept me as I am. I'm around, but never in any role.'

'I am always made welcome at church, but they would like me to be more involved,' says Sally, a solicitor, married to a curate.'But the Vicar has done such a good job of describing the demanding and time-consuming job that I allegedly do, that they rarely pressure me. It would be different if I was at home, I am certain. Anyway, Nick would hate an interfering wife.'

Anne, who is married to a non-stipendiary minister, says, 'I lead our home group if Stephen's away, I lead the children's ministry, I'm an Alpha course co-leader, and I do baptism interviews. At times I feel I do more than he does, because I have more time available, but he has the up-front role and takes the credit! I sometimes grouse but I know this is the way that suits our skills best. We believe in a joint ministry. It's not for everyone, but this is what God wants for us.'

There remains some division over the idea of 'joint ministry'. As one wife, Catherine, wrote to me, 'Shortly after marrying my husband, I was invited to a diocesan-wide gathering of clergy wives, at which I met 30 or so women of varying backgrounds and ages. I was struck by how many envisaged themselves as their husbands' co-workers in the parish, speaking not of "his" but of "our" ministry. A few even used language such as "when we were at theological college" though it was clear that these women had not themselves been students. For the most part, they had assumed some form of parish leadership and were deeply invested in helping their husbands make a success of their ministry.'

In *Holy Matrimony?*, Kirk and Leary quote the Bishop of Bradford, speaking on this question during a General Synod debate in 1993 on clergy marriage.'At least twice in past years when there has been a vacancy I have received a very strong request, if not demand, from a

PCC to interview the wife of any prospective new incumbent,' he said. 'Search the Book of Common Prayer or the ASB as you will; there is no service for the ordination of the wife.' This was made more difficult, he said, by clergy and their wives talking about 'our' ministry. 'I think I know what they sometimes mean [but] I believe that those who talk about "our" ministry are in danger of encouraging precisely that misconceived idea that the wife of a clergyman is *ex officio* some kind of minister with a clear role in the parish. She is not.'

Kirk and Leary write, 'The reality is that something close to the stereotype [of the clergy wife] does exist, but that she belongs increasingly to the generation of women now in their fifties or older, who were not necessarily brought up to go out to work, were often themselves daughters of the vicarage, and for whom self-sacrifice was the expectation and the norm. A large number of marriage breakdowns among clergy couples occur in this age group, because the self has become disabled through deprivation. The younger clergy wife who is utterly dedicated with her husband's vocation can still be found ... but such examples are rare, and usually to be found among those with fairly extreme conservative evangelico-charismatic tendencies.'

They go on to say, 'The more a wife can be separated from the orbit of her husband's ministry, the more the clergy couple will increase their ability to relate to each other as people, and not solely through the medium of "their" ministry which ... can lead to the danger of breakdown when that medium no longer exists.'

There is a world of difference, however, between inappropriate absorption (I have even heard one older clergy wife, a lay-woman, refer to 'our ordination') and having a sense of joint enterprise, as an essential element of marriage. Sometimes, perhaps, the picture is muddied by misunderstanding. For example, if I refer to 'our' church, I mean no more by this than the church family of which

I, my husband and children are a part. Similarly, during the selection process which preceded my husband's most recent appointment, I was invited to accompany him to his interview in the parish. I happily did so, not because I see myself as his co-worker, but because I wanted to look round the house and the village, and meet some members of the local community, so that if he was offered the job, we could make an informed decision together about our future. Though my antennae were working overtime, I did not have any sense of being interviewed or vetted by the parish.

This ambiguity of interpretation is summed up by one clergy wife, Felicity, who, when I asked if she was involved in her partner's ministry, replied, 'Yes, profoundly, as his wife, partner, mother of his child, washer of his clothes, gardener, housekeeper and lover. I am a regular member of his congregation, and we pray together as we share a common spirituality. Since we share the same space, I am therefore very influenced by the pace of his life. Also, of course, I get to know people, and so I am involved with their grief and joy. But I am not officially involved in any Church institutions or committees.'

EXPECTATIONS IN THE PARISH

When we moved recently, I was introduced to the wife of a retired Methodist minister living nearby. We were discussing parish life. 'Are there any expectations of you?' she asked. 'Do you have expectations in the Church of England?' I laughed; I confess I had thought that expectations were something of an Anglican speciality.

The official line in the Church of England is that there should be no particular expectations of the partners of the clergy. *Faith in the City*, published in 1985, reported in its section on clergy families: 'Some wives' main concern was their own employment, while other wives did much more as unpaid voluntary workers assisting their husbands. And there was a variety of other arrangements designed to suit the circumstances of individual households. We note these various alternatives and we see them all as equally valid. We subscribe to the unexceptionable view that the way a clergyman relates to other members of his household is a matter for him personally, and there should be no expectations from us about the particular way clergy wives organize their lives.'

The authors of the sister report, *Faith in the Countryside*, wrote in 1990: 'It makes an enormous difference if the clergy spouse is in paid employment, since this not only adds to the family income, but also provides a separate role outside the parish. This is more significant for wives of clergy since they are usually expected to play a particular parish role. The [project] found that 71 per cent of rural church people felt that clergy wives have or should have a significant supportive role to play in the parish. Even in the general population the survey found that 56 per cent of people felt the same.'

The report continues, 'Evidence suggests that clergy wives in rural parishes may be particularly vulnerable. Some younger clergy wives have been taken by surprise at the level of personal hostility which can be directed towards them when their husbands pursue an unpopular course of action. On the other hand, wives may be approached by people with problems who want to talk to a woman. This can be a very positive role for those who are happy to accept it, but it puts great strain on those who feel unable to respond, or who do not want to be used as an alternative to their husbands.'

As the report makes clear, theory (that partners are not officially part of a minister's ministry) and practice do not always match up. While a number of clergy wives I spoke to said they were unaware of there being any expectations from their husband's parish, many others felt there was pressure to fulfil a certain role. Clergy husbands seem to be exempt from this (see Chapter 8). The degree to which a parish has any such expectations seems to depend on a combination of different factors, all of which may be interrelated. First, the expectations the parish has of its minister, and the degree to which ideas about lay ministry have been embraced. Second, past experience of a clergy spouse (what I call the 'Rebecca syndrome', after Daphne du Maurier's novel about a second wife who is haunted by the memory of her dead predecessor). Third, the particular character and socio-economic make-up of the parish.

Much has been written on the development of lay ministry in recent years. Robin Greenwood, in his book *Transforming Priesthood*, wrote that, for Anglicans in particular, 'the combined forces of pragmatism and theology at the close of the twentieth century are sweeping [the Church] inexorably to a fundamentally new concept of the parochial ministry.' In spite of great strides forward in the 1990s to encourage lay ministry, he argues, there remains in many churches 'a disproportionate emphasis on the role of the clergy to the detriment of the whole body of the Church'. He calls for a rejection of the inherited model of a benign priesthood shepherding a passive flock, and for this to be replaced with a ministry of the whole people, where the laity and clergy animate each other.

The extent to which a particular parish or church has embraced the concept of lay ministry filters down to a clergy family. The more that lay ministry is happening within a church, the greater chance the clergy spouse will have of being 'just another member of the congregation'. A more passive congregation will expect more of its minister, and will be far less likely to take on the running of the areas presumed in past years to come within the sphere of the clergy wife. Pauline, the wife of a Methodist minister told me, 'When we first arrived here seven years ago, I was a practising Roman Catholic. But they still expected me to lead the women's groups.' Another wife, Sheila, says, 'I've tried and tried to get someone else to take on the crèche rota and other responsibilities, but with no success. They also rely on me for music. If we want to take a Sunday off, it's not just a matter of finding someone to take the service, but whether they can survive without me playing the organ. And I am expected to attend various meetings and gatherings, even though I work full-time.'

The Rebecca syndrome appears to sum up the sorts of expectations that do exist. One wife told me the story of friends of hers who were looking round a parish as a possible curacy for the husband. Someone said to the wife, 'The last curate's wife ran the music group. Is this something you think you could take on?' 'Not really,' she said, 'I'm afraid I'm not musical. I don't actually play the piano or anything.' 'Well,' came the reply, 'you've got a year, couldn't you learn?'

A number of wives said that they had experienced similar assumptions, that they would fill the gap left by the previous vicar's wife, 'though they are gradually accepting that my gifts are different', said one, kindly. This can, of course, work both ways. 'I imagine some think it odd I don't go to the Mothers Union, or anything,' says Vanessa. 'But I think some people are probably quite glad; the previous incumbent's wife was a little *too* actively involved in her husband's work for many parishioners. Anything I do in church or in the parish grows out of my own interests or expertise, as with any member of the congregation.'

'When we first arrived, all I kept hearing was that Jill had done this, that or the other,' says Caroline. 'Not only did she have five children – all perfectly behaved, of course – but she was a brilliant organizer and ran everything there was to run in the church, the school and the community. It took me five or six months to discover that actually everyone was terrified of her.'

More happily, a growing number of spouses say that they are unaware of there being any expectations of them taking on any particular role. 'Traditional' clergy wives, who offer their services full-time to the parish, are increasingly becoming the exception rather than the rule, enabling those who follow to tread their own paths more easily. 'The last vicar's wife was teaching full-time and did nothing in the parish – she did me a huge favour,' said Julie. Another wife, Fiona, says, 'I am very lucky with our present church – having had no vicar and vicar's wife for nine years there were no shoes to step into. I am not aware of any expectations, though I am sure they would be disappointed if I didn't attend or support activities.'

It is apparent, however, that the experience of expectations does vary significantly from one situation to another. 'Now William is a college chaplain, there are no expectations of me, but in the parish they were high,' says Alice. 'But these were on a practical rather than spiritual level – things like regular coffee mornings and organizing jumble sales. The only exception to that was wanting me to be Enrolling Member of the Mothers Union (which I declined); I'm still not sure which category that was.'

'No one has ever said anything,' says Caroline, who lives in a small village. 'But being in a rural parish, I do feel very visible, that what I do or don't do is always noticed.' In contrast, Rhiannon, who lives in an urban priority area (UPA), says, 'There are no expectations of me, but this is an inner-city church, where many are from a non-church culture. But I have my own ministry, anyway; I'm a school governor, an Alpha group leader, I'm involved in counselling, running youth clubs, and preaching occasionally.'

'I haven't been a "clergy wife" for long but the atmosphere in the church makes a big difference,' says Sue, who also lives in an inner-city parish. 'In the first church where Frank was a curate it was a very traditional church, and it was awful. It is fine where we are now, and the congregation do not have any big expectations of me, so I can more or less act as I want. I am nervous about going to another church, when – after three years – we have finally organized a good working and living situation for ourselves.'

EXPECTATIONS FROM WITHIN

The authors of *Faith in the Countryside* wrote, 'Perhaps more surprising [than the expectations of the parish] was the survey of clergy themselves, which found that although a significant number were keen not to assign a role to their spouses, a greater number did expect or prescribe certain roles. The dominant theme was that clergy wives should have a background, supportive or "wifely" role.'

A number of those I interviewed testified to this. 'I feel William would like me to have a much higher profile,' says Alice. 'I try to be involved as much as I can be, where my strengths lie, and what will fit in with the children, but this is quite limited. I am certainly looking forward to being more involved when the children are older.'

'Charles would like me to be involved alongside him,' Melanie, a mother of four young children told me. 'But I think when one of you is totally immersed, it's better for the other not to jump in too, and risk both drowning. But I could be more of a prayer support than I am.'

Others admitted to having to struggle with their partner's wishes. 'I know he would be happier if I were more involved,' says Julie. 'But in the end, he respects my wish to retain my individuality and recognizes that my gifts and talents lie elsewhere.' 'If there were any occasions when it would be appropriate for me to attend and Richard really wanted me to, then I would,' says Ruth.

'Otherwise I feel these are choices he has made, and they should not automatically include me. I do not share his outgoing personality, and a constant round of social events would be a source of great stress to me.'

Some clergy spouses experienced expectations from other clergy, especially during their partner's curacy. An older generation of wives may also feel threatened by a different approach taken by a younger clergy spouse. 'It is more accepted now that we are individuals rather than an unpaid extra,' Jeanette, a Methodist in her thirties told me. 'But it's some of the retired ministers' wives are the ones who expect most of the younger ones.'

'I am not actively involved in my husband's ministry,' says Catherine. 'I believe that the best contribution I can make to his parish is to concentrate on caring for him and the health of our marriage. Only once have I been directly told that it would be wise for me to take a more active role in the parish. Our Rector's wife advised me that it would be good for me to be "seen" more, and urged me to join the group of women who prepare the church on Saturdays for worship. She may well have offered this advice because of disapproval others were expressing about my low profile within the parish.'

'There are more expectations from Alan's boss and his wife than from the church,' says Janet, a curate's wife. 'For instance, the curate's wife is automatically on the PCC and the women's work committee.'

Another side of the ambivalence some clergy feel about the role of their wives is revealed by Anne, who is married to a non-stipendiary minister. 'The vicar is the one person who doesn't have any expectations of me,' she says. 'But that's because the more I do, the more he feels his wife should do, and he's not happy about this! I'm aware this is a very bald statement but it is a fact.'

And what of our own expectations, of ourselves? Why, I asked myself recently – when I have two young children, work three days a week, spend a lot of time taking phone messages and answering the door, not to mention my share of the domestic burden, when I regularly take my turn on the Sunday school, reading and coffee rotas, when I am on the church social committee – why do I still sometimes catch myself wondering if this might not be enough?

Many other wives I spoke to echoed feelings of guilt. 'I feel that I am free to choose the roles that I take on,' says Charlotte. 'But I have had to overcome the guilt of not doing jobs where there is a need, such as leading the toddler group or cleaning the church.' Another, Jo, says, 'I couldn't do any less, when so many other busy people give up so much of their time.'

Others were very clear at the outset about their own expectations. 'My mother-in-law's example as a vicar's wife was my main preparation for the whole thing,' says Wendy. 'I was so determined that I was not going to be like her – always putting herself last, thinking everyone's needs were more important than her own, and being so self-effacing that she was walked on – that I've made sure I've gone my own way.'

'Just be yourself,' our Rector's wife told me when my husband was first a curate. I am sure she was right; no other approach makes any sort of sense. But it's having the confidence and taking the time to find out what that means in practice that is sometimes the problem.

2

WORK

The last few decades have seen huge changes to the working world. From the boom of the 1980s to the recession of the early 1990s, hand-in-hand with creeping unemployment, Britain's workforce has undergone a radical reshaping in recent years which has affected us all. We are left with a high degree of job insecurity, the growth of part-time work, deregulation and a boom in short-term contracts, the longest working hours in Europe and an environment where work-related stress is now deemed to be the most serious health-hazard British workers face.

It is against this backdrop that the clergy live out their vocations. What choices are clergy families making about work, and how do they fit their working lives around each other? Many of the tensions they experience may be shared by others in secular jobs; others are more specific to the ordained ministry.

THE WORK OF THE CLERGY

Irrespective of whether the clergy view their job as a vocation, a career or a profession, their priestly task still constitutes work. The clergy have not been immune from the current upheaval in the working world. The twentieth century has seen a significant shift in the position of the clergy within society, and a steady erosion of the old conventions and understanding about their role. Confronted with the financial pressures, and the ongoing squeeze on the deployment of ministers, together with recent developments in theological thought, today's clergy face the reappraisal of the entire concept of ministry.

'It is probably true that there is no longer a single confident style or role for the clergy. This is due to changes in society ... ordination training has to deal with the inescapable plurality of views of what the ordained ministry is. This plurality can cause anxiety,' reported the Church of England's Advisory Board of Ministry (ABM) in 1992. In 1993, another ABM report found that 'the impact of [social change] on the Church and its ministers varies, but in many situations they find old ways of relating to society unworkable and new opportunities opening up. A particular challenge attaches to pastoral care and the giving of counsel in the face of increasingly complex ethical problems and the wider range of choice exercised by many, notably but not exclusively in the context of personal relationship and marriage.'

Faith in the Countryside, meanwhile, found that 'for many rural clergy, the principal problems of ministry arise from the fact that they find themselves trapped between the realities of modern multi-parish ministry, the traditional expectations of the laity formed possibly as much as two generations ago, and a perception of priesthood which was formed during the period of their own training. In essence the model of ministry by which many rural clergy operate is inappropriate for the structures in which they are required to work.'

Within this changing context, the clergy are still called (in the ASB ordinal) 'to be messengers, watchmen, and stewards of the Lord ... to teach and to admonish, to feed and to provide for the Lord's family, to search for his children in the wilderness of this world's temptations and to guide them through its confusions, so that they may be saved by Christ for ever.'

The work of the clergy is thus rarely straightforward, and as full of potential tensions as it is rewards. For most people, their work (or lack of it) shapes their lives, and this is nowhere more so than for the clergy and their families, only here it is intensified by the fact that all but a very few of Britain's clergy work from home.

One of the problematic aspects of the job – which comes up on a regular, almost cyclical basis – is the difficulty of achieving manageable working hours. The spouses I spoke to told of their partner's day stretching from morning until late at night; one said her husband regularly worked 16 hours a day, 6 days a week. Many of those in secular work would feel they also struggled to maintain a healthy balance between work and family life. However, the problem for the clergy is compounded not only by work intruding into the domestic sphere, but also by the difficulty of imposing any sort of structure on an essentially unstructured job.

In an article in the *Church Times* in 1996, a clergy husband expressed his resentment of 'those workaholics in the Church of England who regularly treat their own family life as second to work' (referring to other clergy, rather than to his own wife). 'Of course, I understand that there are emergencies. A recent call at half-past midnight from a distressed parishioner was not a cause of complaint from me,' he wrote.'[But] my basic principle is: we need time when work can get lost unless there's a genuine emergency. "Genuine emergency" means death, dying, visitation by the spirit of Zool, and so on, not a dispute over flowers, hymn choice or who has the safe key. For the sanity of everyone, and to toe the biblical line, clergy should have one day a week that is totally free from the otherwise never-ending pressures of work.

'By the same principle, shouldn't the working day have some similar boundaries? I've watched members of

34

the clergy work too many consecutive three-session [morning, afternoon *and* evening] days. It's not good for them, for their families or ultimately for the extension of the kingdom of God. Flog a live horse and you'll soon have a dead one.'

Responses came pouring in to the letters page. One reader wrote asking what working hours NSMs, lay readers and other active church members should aim for, if stipendiary clergy 'only' worked a 12-session week. Another, a (male) vicar, thundered, 'Do clergy really have a fixed hour when they become incommunicado, by turning on the telephone answering machine? What do they do about the desperate caller at the door: refuse to answer the frantic ringing on the bell and hope that he or she will go away? Is a maximum of 44 hours of work a week feasible? What sort of clergy work half-time like that? In a busy inner-urban parish, 12 hours a day and 7 days a week is standard . . . I have not had a Sunday off, let alone a Saturday, in seven years. What am I supposed to do? Shut up shop for a week? . . . The trouble with some of our up-and-coming young clergy is that they have become besotted with the idea of *le weekend*. The day off is sacrosanct. Well, it isn't.'

Others, in turn, rightly pointed out that time off and holidays were, of course, essential to the spiritual, physical and mental health of every priest, as well as a biblically-based principle. Others, elsewhere, have pointed to the high incidence of clergy stress and marriage breakdown, which are never helped by one half of the couple working ridiculous hours.

None the less, the clergy seem to find it very hard to achieve a reasonable balance between their working and non-working hours. The task is, after all, a never-ending one, which could never be finished, however many hours of the day or night were given over to it. The clergy themselves are highly motivated by their sense of calling and service, and often overstretched in terms of human

35

resources. No doubt some ministers are more organized in their work than others, and some are more committed to drawing boundaries between work and leisure, but I have yet to meet a clergy family for whom the issue of working hours, and time off, is completely resolved.

Many families find the transition from a five-day working week to full-time ministry a difficult adjustment, with the loss of weekends, only a single weekday off, and the endless evening commitments. Some see their Sundays transformed from a family day, albeit centred around church attendance, to a 14-hour marathon, when the longest glimpse the rest of the family have of their clergy partner or parent occurs while they are in the pew. 'For me, Saturdays are the worst of all,' Rachel, a vicar's wife with very young children told me. 'I was used to the idea that Sundays would be taken up with church activities; they already were, really. But I hadn't realized how isolated I'd feel on Saturdays, when everyone else is doing family things, and I'm on my own with the children, yet again.'

I have experienced that loneliness myself, and have often resented not having a proper family day together – since the children began school, a mid-week day off no longer offers a proper substitute. It can be very hard work, being the one at home alone, weekend after weekend, and at times affords a glimmer of understanding into the lot of lone parents. The antisocial working hours also make it difficult to keep up with old friends and the wider family. Aside from the obvious impossibility of going away for weekends, even Saturday nights can be a problem. The choice is between driving back through the night before a very early start on Sunday morning or never taking up any invitations to weddings, parties, college reunions or other events.

Others talked of the 'constant struggle' to get the balance right between work and family life. 'We've come closer to the right balance since Tom became a college chaplain,' said Diana. 'In the parish we found it very difficult.'

'In busy weeks, work takes over completely. It's also hard that Henry works from home, because it's difficult to know when work ends. He seems to work all day and all evening. Basically, I would just like to see my husband a bit more. I don't like him having to work a six-day week', says Louise, voicing a complaint I heard again and again.'We are constantly under pressure of time,' says Jo. 'I think it's unfair for David to work three sessions a day and have only one day off. But he has to work these hours to fit the work in.'

'One of the aspects of his job I find most difficult to accept is that Michael has only one day of the week off,' agrees Catherine. 'Since he often has to spend part of this day on non-parochial tasks that have accumulated during the week, we have little time together simply to relax. Only rarely can we escape from the parish for an entire day. I do not comprehend why the Church contin-ues in the belief that the clergy need only one day off a week, when the rest of society has long acknowledged that so little leisure time is unhealthy.'

I know of some clergy who have overturned this standard arrangement, by insisting on taking two days off per week – 'one to do the jobs, the other to relax', one vicar told me. However creative, this may not be easy to organize, and may well meet resistance from other clergy as well as parishioners. It would certainly be easier to arrange within a team ministry than for a solo minister with several churches, and also, of course, depends on the spouse's working hours, if the time off is going to be spent together.

'It's something to be worked at continuously,' says Caroline. 'Circumstances change and people's needs change. I'd like it to be more generally recognized that clergy need time off at home for themselves, their families, for domestic chores and servicing in addition to that one day off per week.'

'It is hard not to resent the constant demands from needy people,' says Alice. 'Learning to say "No" is only part of the scenario. The other is deciding which things to say "No" to. It is easy to be pious about this and let God lead, but in practice, tough choices have to be made.'

The practicalities can be stark. 'There are particular difficulties for Stephen as an NSM,' says Anne. 'Many of the people in the parish – and the Parish Priest – think of him as a curate, which he is not. As the Vicar lives in the other parish, Stephen is often the first call to people here. It was hard for them to find him not available during the day. In the end we had to make strong statements about exactly how much he did, and when. He does not visit, for example, or take funerals. People come to him by appointment now.'

Others, however, value the flexibility the unstructured hours afford. Some home-based spouses pointed out that having lunch together on weekdays was a bonus not shared by many couples. One wife, Jean, told me, 'One brilliant aspect of being married to a vicar is that Tim can often be home at the children's tea-time. You don't get that in many jobs. And before they went to school, having a day off mid-week was great – you miss the crowds if you go out.'

There are other advantages in the flexibility. At one stage, when Ben was a curate, and I had a part-time job, he was able to meet the children from school on the three days I worked. When I returned at 6 o'clock, we had a family meal together before he began work again. However, even this took some negotiating; a colleague within Ben's team (who himself worked extremely long hours) expressed some reservations about him taking those hours 'off'. One or two parishioners raised eyebrows over the arrangement. 'Exactly when was the curate's day off?' asked one person. 'Could I approach him on parish business, if I met him in the street with the children?' asked another. There was a feeling that, somehow, the children were more properly my responsibility than his.

Another wife, Marion, told me that her own return to work had the positive effect of forcing a structure on her husband's working life. 'When I went back to work, we had to sit down and evolve a pattern to the day,' she says. 'Otherwise he'd just keep on and on working. It forced him into a routine, and we found that very helpful as a family.'

A number of others expressed resentment that their partner's work took over their lives. 'My husband would say we have the right balance between work and time off, but I don't think so,' says Katie. 'When we got married, I accepted that his work was of primary importance, and realized that family life would come second. Work has taken over more and more time, though. Sometimes I feel if we all moved out for a week he wouldn't notice – till he needed clean shirts, bless him! I feel like a housekeeper much of the time.'

Although in many families today the domestic burden is likely to be shared more equally between partners than it was a generation ago, this appears to be less frequently the case with clergy families. There remains a feeling among many that the work of the priest is more important than anything else, that the priest in the family is about his or her Father's business, and must be enabled to carry this out.

'I don't feel Henry gives my "work" as full-time wife and mother much weight,' says Louise. 'The Church is always first, and it is easy to resent it.' 'As a wife and new mother I felt *very* resentful of Peter's work,' says Wendy. 'He was out doing the Lord's work, and I was at home doing very badly (or so I thought) trying to keep a tidy house and look after two babies. However much I knew in my head that I was doing a very valuable job that I

39

wouldn't want anyone else to do for me, I still felt that what Peter was doing was far more important and interesting.'

Janet Finch's research for *Married to the Job?*, although carried out some years ago, points to the motivation that still underlies the domestic set-up for many clergy families. 'Wives of men who undertake noble endeavours (or perhaps more accurately, men with wives who *believe* they are engaged in noble endeavours) may find that the potential competition between work and family, far from being expressed in conflict between husband and wife, results in the husband being given *more* space to get on with the great work. A wife who sees work taking over her husband's whole life, and who endorses the legitimacy of its claims upon him, may well respond by taking on *all* responsibility for domestic tasks, leaving him free to concentrate on his work. This certainly seems to be the case for clergy couples. Although one might imagine that home-based work with no set working times would result in a husband taking on *more* responsibility for domestic work and child-care, the opposite seems to be the case.'

My own belief is that this imbalance is worth fighting against, and hard. The precise allocation of domestic tasks is not the issue; but that they are shared is. Invaluable as the priestly work may be, this does not mean that anyone else's time is less valuable. Nor would I want my children growing up with the idea that their father's work as a clergyman is sacrosanct (and thus any other calling second-rate, a highly suspect theological concept if ever there was one) or that it should automatically take precedence over the nitty-gritty of domestic life.

SPOUSES' WORK

'Did you have a job before you were married?' someone once asked me, when we arrived in a parish. I was taken aback, as I viewed the interruption in my working life as temporary, not permanent, and caused (willingly) by motherhood rather than marriage. I had in fact supported Ben financially through part of his time at theological college, and was planning to return to part-time work when the children were a little older. I was also surprised as the woman who asked was a retired teacher who had worked for much of her own married life. Yet it became clear in the course of the conversation that, in her eyes, my 'work' now was to support my husband and she assumed that this was what I would do from now on.

Far more clergy wives have their own careers now than a generation ago. (Clergy husbands barely merit a mention here, I'm afraid; it is nearly always assumed that they already have a 'real' job.) Those in my survey who were not working were, with very few exceptions, taking a break from paid jobs to care for young children. For those in employment, their reasons for working (if reasons are required) varied from actively pursuing a career, to getting out of the parish, to purely meeting financial demands. Their fields of work ranged from teaching, public relations, publishing, accountancy, nursing, journalism, counselling, lecturing, speech therapy, hospital administration, to art and law.

'When I work I feel less resentful of the way that the job as vicar takes over our lives,' says Linda. Mary, who took a part-time job as soon as her four children were at school, says, 'My role in the wider community as a school nurse has given me a greater sense of balance. It has both helped us financially and given us "space in our togetherness".' 'Work serves two purposes at the moment,' says Jean, a supply teacher. 'First, money for extras and, second, keeping me informed so that it is easier to go back later.' 'I'm happy to be out at work, so that I'm not constantly having to make excuses and trying to cope with needy people when there is no hope of seeing Stephen immediately,' says Anne.

Some wives regard their work as being equally

important as their partner's; a surprisingly high number as less so. This was reflected in the sense that the priestly task was somehow the 'real work' in the family, but also in the reality of living in tied accommodation. 'Our jobs are of equal status,' says Emma. 'But as our home goes with his appointment, and that affects where we live, and where the children go to school, I think we should consider his first.' 'I look on my work as equally important, but it would generally be regarded as secondary to Christopher's,' says Sheila, who, like her husband, is nearing retirement. 'He would regard it as such, I believe! Except for the financial angle, as I now earn as much as he does.' 'His is God's work, mine is not,' says Liz, a part-time accountant. 'I see his ministry as being of greater importance to any work I could ever do,' says Katie, a mother of teenagers and at home full-time.

To some of the younger generation of clergy spouses, it comes as a surprise that their working lives might come under public scrutiny, yet, amazingly, this still seems to happen. In Mary Loudon's book *Revelations*, for which she interviewed a number of Church of England clergy at length, one vicar tells this story from his own experience. 'There is an insane and quite, quite ridiculous expectation that people have of clergy families. For instance, not long after we got here, Dorothy got a job. We had one child at college, two at school, and I had a telephone call from an elderly member of the congregation who was disgusted that my wife worked as a domestic assistant at Bishopscourt Old People's Home, and proceeded for the next half-hour to tell me off about that. Being fairly green in the job, and not wanting to be too offensive, I took this on the jaw for quite some considerable time. My patience finally ran out, and I said, "Look, I'm awfully sorry, but if my wife didn't work, we wouldn't eat!" She then had the effrontery to give me a lecture about my personal finances.'

Other wives have, on occasion, met hostility and

disapproval about their working from members of their husband's congregations. One remembers the disapproval of her voluntary work as a city councillor and member of various pressure groups; another met with annoyance that she would no longer be able to attend or chair day-time meetings when she took a part-time job. Another (a vicar's daughter) says, 'To people of my mother's generation, to say you are going back to work and you're leaving your pre-school children with a childminder is just anathema. You might as well say you're going to leave them with a heroin addict.'

Another says she has met with a complete lack of interest in her job from anyone in the congregation – something she finds hurtful, as her work is very important to her. Someone else says that while she is very happy not to be working, she feels sure there would be 'a certain amount of disappointment' if she chose not to be a full-time clergy wife. A third finds it necessary to make it plain that she works part-time only, so as to allow time for some Church commitments.

Others encounter support and enthusiasm from the parish. Emma, a mother of three who started a university degree shortly after her husband was ordained, says, 'Our first church showed great interest – and admiration – of me as a full-time student. This church has been equally supportive since I got my degree and started teaching.' Jo, a music teacher at home with young children, says that one member of the congregation has recently offered her some piano pupils, and another passed on details of a job vacancy to her. Another wife, Linda, says, 'Most people see the stresses of our lifestyle, and think it's very healthy for me to have an outside job.'

My own husband's parish has not questioned the fact that I have a job, despite the last vicar's wife being someone who was extremely busy helping in the parish. The only difficulty is that, as I work from home at the

43

moment, I can be in, but not available. I have had to explain to one or two people that if I am at my desk, I will not be answering the telephone or the door; it is just as if I am in the office. Although I have Ben's full support in this, and I know I would not be able to carry out my work otherwise, I am none the less conscious that some people might find this hard to take.

Other wives I spoke to echoed this with similar experiences. Vanessa, who runs a small nursery garden from home, says, 'I think people are interested in what I do, but generally there's a lack of understanding that if I am home-based, I have to work on the garden and plants and am not necessarily available. There is also some expectation that I am engaged in charitable work – to help church funds, for example – and a lack of appreciation that I actually need to earn some money.'

Catherine, working on a Ph.D., told me, 'A small number of parishioners have expressed an interest in my dissertation and have offered me encouragement. Most, however, don't understand the purpose or requirements of the work. I suspect that, because I work at home and am unpaid, many perceive that what I am doing is neither exacting nor particularly important. I also suspect that my minimal involvement in parish life would be slightly better understood if I had a "proper job".'

The advantages of working from home, she says (and I would agree), are that she has the chance to see her husband for lunch, and at odd times during the day. 'Were I working outside the home, I would see him far too infrequently, as his evenings are largely taken up with parish meetings or visits and, of course, he works weekends.'

Their partner's working hours puts many people off taking on work themselves or restricts them in the sort of job they can do. Personally, I am not prepared to sacrifice a weekly day off together, and Saturdays here are too often interrupted to offer a realistic alternative to a weekday. This is our choice, but for as long as my husband remains in parish ministry, this limits the sort of job I am available to do. Any spouse with a full-time, Monday to Friday job has the same problem managing a day off with their clergy partner.

'I don't feel that I can separate myself from Alan's work, and therefore it must affect my priorities,' Janet told me. 'I wouldn't take on full-time work, because we would never see each other. There is a sadness in that, and struggles ensue, but for everything you gain there is always sacrifice.' 'I work a couple of days a week, but any more than that, and we feel we are ships that pass in the night,' says Wendy. 'We always take one day off together. It is a reasonable balance, but never perfect.'

Another wife, Joanne, is frustrated that she has to work at all. 'The stipend is so appalling, I have to work to make ends meet,' she says. 'If only the pay was more realistic, I wouldn't have to work and this would alleviate some of the other pressures on us all as a family.' Marjorie, in her fifties and a mother of six, believes that their family life had only been possible because she has always stayed at home. 'But having me there full-time doesn't make up for all the evenings the children spent without their father,' she says.

Another restriction is the ever-present threat of re-location. This is not, of course, a situation unique to clergy families, though perhaps the fact that the family is required to live in one partner's workplace (rather than, say, half-way between two jobs) makes it slightly more acute.

'When I married, I moved to the parish where my husband was working,' says Catherine. 'In the five years since we've been married, we have moved five times. Though, in all but one instance, I believed the moves were worth making, they have taken a decided toll on my academic work, which I do regret. Whatever work I under-take in the future, my husband and I will regard both as equally important, and any decision we make about moving will have to be made from that perspective.'

'We've moved three times for his work, and I feel angry about this sometimes,' says Felicity, who is an artist and teacher. 'My work has always been central to my life and since marriage I have had to let go of a good deal – our geographical location, the time available for me, restrictions on our social life and energy due to the demands of the job, restrictions on the time available for my own work. I feel that my work is not considered important by the Church, or even considered at all. Even I feel that it is "less worthy", but I work on because I've had to, because I love it.'

It has to be said that the institutional Church has not always been very considerate about spouses' work when suggesting job moves for its clergy. Anecdotal evidence suggests this may be improving, although some wives record being made to feel greedy or selfish if they hold out for their own jobs or other family considerations when looking at a move. Some, however, manage to be creative with job moves. 'We've moved just as much for my job as for Rob's,' says Karen. 'This time it was for him, but we have an informal arrangement to swap whose job dictates the next move. It's my turn next, all things being equal.' Siobhan, a clergy wife of 30 years, says, 'When we last moved, Philip made it quite clear at his interview that one of the ways he felt God was calling him to this particular parish was because I had just been offered a job here in London. They were fine about it.'

Most of those who are in employment of any sort today are under enormous pressure to work long and hard. As another generation of children grows up without ever having heard the Christian message, as increasing numbers face poverty and family disintegration, the task facing the clergy looms large. But my own conclusion is that we *all* need to be more creative about our working lives, wherever possible, and work towards a balance between work and non-work that allows for family life, leisure time and recreation, and is spiritually, emotionally and physically healthy. The clergy need to remember that their priestly task extends to their own family, and be prepared to let go of the tyranny of work. The working lives of all dual-career families need to become, wherever possible, a positive rather than an oppressive or competitive thing. Equally, the contributions of spouses who choose not to go into the workplace need to be valued, too.

There are different stages in the life of a couple, whether or not they have children, and the organization of work, whether paid or domestic, should, ideally, be an organic process, one that can be re-examined and, if necessary, changed at regular intervals. Our lives are complicated and multidimensional, and our time as families is precious. Just because everybody else appears to be working long hours does not mean it is necessarily a good thing. The great thing about the job of the clergy is that, within certain restrictions, the hours and shape of an individual ministry can be flexible. Ideally, it offers a great opportunity to test the waters and try out alternative working structures that are more, not less, life-enhancing. Work is, after all, only one part of our lives, and only one part of a priest's ministry. We could generalize here and say that, while most men have jobs, most women have jobs that fit in. What we all need, of course, both men and women, is jobs that fit in with life. The Church could be leading the way towards change.

3

MARRIAGE AND
PARTNERSHIP

Marriage, hand in hand with our partner's vocation, is
what made us clergy spouses. Whether we married
before or after our partner's ordination, we are in some
sense part of that vocation, if only by default. Equally,
marriage is part of the reality of the married priest's
vocation. This chapter will look at some of the tensions
inherent in clergy marriages, the particular stresses and
expectations placed on them, and the crucial question
of what it means in practice to try and live out both
marriage and ordination vows.

MARRIAGE AND MINISTRY

It is difficult to disentangle the concepts of marriage and
ministry; they cannot help but impinge on each other.
When a vacancy arises, the vast majority of parishes in
the Church of England, we are told, will specify – however unjustly – a preference for 'a family man'. This,
together with the fact that parishes must house the
whole family, and not just the appointed candidate,
means that the existence (or otherwise) of a spouse and
children on an applicant's C.V. assumes a significance

far greater than it would for almost any other job application.

Inevitably tension arises from the fact that the more time and energy the clergy give to their work, the less time there will be left to devote to their marriage relationship and children, and yet if these relationships are in bad shape, their priestly ministry cannot help but be affected. Rosemary Lury sums this up in her contribution to *Married to the Church?*: 'No one can function effectively in their job if their domestic life is in turmoil, and this is particularly so for a priest, I believe, for his marriage is so much more public. I felt that because our marriage was strained, I was hindering Anthony in his work with others. I thought I was being unfair in asking him to spend more time with the family, because it would prevent him from preparing his sermon, reading, praying, visiting and so on.'

The picture is further complicated by the kind of moral pressure felt by many clergy partners, wives especially, to devote considerable time and energy to supporting the priest who is doing a highly valued (and, within Church circles, highly respected) job. The idea that a high degree of self-sacrifice 'for the sake of the Church' is demanded of wives is difficult to shed. As one happily married clergy wife wrote to me, 'The potential for abuse of moral and religious imperatives in a clergy marriage is huge.'

In his book *Transforming Priesthood*, Robin Greenwood calls on the clergy to give attention to their marriages, at a time when the rate of marital breakdown is so high in Britain. 'In order to be a personal embodiment of the link between the "spiritual" and the "practical" elements of human living, the priest needs to be in a position to attempt to model not only priesthood, but a marriage partner, parent, friend, and member of the local and world communities . . . A sizeable proportion of clergy becomes entrenched in a narrow field of vision and activity in which most other relations are abandoned "for the sake of the Church". In those called to witness in the public office of president within the local church and wider community, some evidence of a new balance is required, towards participation in the untidy relations of family, community and society. Questions surrounding the priest's suitability to hold the position of president in a community must surely include her observable capacity to communicate and to negotiate, to assess and adjust her own performance, as well as to handle alcohol, anger, money, sexuality and time.'

Expectations of marriage itself have, of course, changed enormously in the course of the twentieth century, and perhaps particularly fast over the last 30 years, partly as a result of the impact of the 1960s and the development of feminist thought. There has been a significant shift in the expectation of what marriage can and should deliver, and the more traditional 'functional' style of marriage has, by and large, given way to the 'companionate' style of marriage now predominant in our culture. Personal and sexual fulfilment is now seen as a right, and friendship, intimacy and support are required elements of a good marriage. The majority of couples, however, now co-habit before marrying, and an increasing number of children are born outside wedlock. We have the highest divorce rate in Europe, and yet we continue to marry.

'The clergy couple is caught in the midst of this shifting scene,' write Kirk and Leary in *Holy Matrimony?*. 'On the one hand, they are "supposed" to represent the traditional values of fidelity and chastity, the Christian teaching of no premarital sex and no divorce, and the public institutionalized marriage of past eras. But while they are "supposed" to stand for all this, to be icons of connubial rectitude, they are also prey to all the influences on, and changes in, marriage during this century ... There is a painful ambiguity in a marriage which must, in its public face, represent an institution and its values, but which –

50

of its very nature – give less space for personal matters than others.'

The tensions between rights and duties, personal fulfilment and commitment, community and individual, are dominant contemporary themes in our culture, and no less so for Christians. A curate's wife told me of a visit by a retired bishop and his wife to the theological college where her husband was training. Talking about their life in ministry, the wife recounted the time when her husband had announced one day that they would be moving to India in three weeks' time, as God had called him there. Immediately the wife began preparations to remove the entire household – they had four very young children – to India, apparently without it ever occurring to her to question her husband's decision.

The young woman who recounted this story was appalled – this model of marriage could not have been further from her own. Indeed, most of us today have an outlook on marriage which is very different from that of previous generations; our models are now likely to embrace concepts of partnership, equality and shared decision-making. If we are Christians, of course, we may have a slightly different slant on this. We are called to be 'other' – to be in the world, but not of the world – but what does that mean in the context of marriage? What can, or should, we expect from marriage? What, for instance, does it mean, to be a 'supportive' wife or husband and, more specifically, a supportive spouse to a minister? Does that entail providing full domestic back-up and getting involved in all sorts of church activities to allow the priest to exercise their ministry or is merely taking a benign interest enough? Does that support flow equally in both directions? Clearly, this is something that every couple works out for themselves, in a wide variety of ways, but if the marriage relationship is so central to ministry, how successfully is this being negotiated in practice today?

The overwhelming majority of those I surveyed were convinced that there were certain stresses that were specific to clergy marriage, something that perhaps not so many would have been willing to admit a generation ago. The stresses they listed were, of course, particular to them, but included the lack of privacy, living with others' expectations and a public identity, lack of time together, the clergy partner working from home, the difficulty of making friends, spiritual warfare, money worries, having to make frequent job moves, and coping with a stream of difficult and demanding people. Overall, two of the commonest themes were living life so publicly and the lifestyle created by the pressures of the job. A third issue, which appears to be a persistent undercurrent, is the whole question of sexuality.

SEXUALITY

Mary Loudon quotes one of the clergy she interviewed for *Revelations* as saying, 'That's the painful bit of the Church at the moment, the fighting about the roles of gays and women, and the fighting's symbolic of fear. Yet it could all be so simple. Maybe I'm naïve, but we're terrified of talking about sexuality, aren't we, and that's what the ordination of women is about. It's about sexuality, about power, about the nature of the Church.'

The Church has struggled with sexuality since the year dot, and that struggle shows no sign of disappearing. The current impassioned debate about homosexuality and Christianity is a prime illustration of the Church's long history of ambivalence about concepts of holiness and sexual expression, soul and body, celibacy and pollution. The wider world, meanwhile, is ready to pounce at every instance of perceived hypocrisy or dithering about sexuality by the Church and its ministers. The public is also, despite itself, tantalized by the very idea of chastity, a classic example being someone like Sister

Wendy Beckett ('the nation's favourite nun'), whose television series has been a runaway success. 'It's that slightly titillating combination of watching a nun hold forth on matters sexual that . . . accounts for much of Sister Wendy's TV success,' wrote one reviewer in 1996. 'Her mention of fluffy pubic hair when describing a Stanley Spencer is legendary.'

It was in an attempt to address some of these questions that the Church of England published *Issues in Human Sexuality* in 1991, although it is often assumed that the report addressed only the question of homosexuality. The Old Testament approach to human sexuality, says the report, was that sexual desire was recognized as a normal and powerful element in both men and women, enjoyed but also 'suspect as in some way incompatible with holiness'. Because being in love is so all-consuming, the report continues, 'the Church has tended to see sexual attraction and activity as particularly hostile to God's due place as the supreme object of human love and the proper controller of all human thought, feeling and conduct.'

The report also says, 'Neither Jesus nor Paul demands celibacy as a condition of Christian discipleship, as certain sects were later to do. Paul indeed explicitly recognizes the strength of sexual desire, and regards marriage as the one divinely ordained place for its physical expression . . . though he sees celibacy as a better state in which to serve the Lord.' It continues, 'From the time of the New Testament onwards it has been expected of those appointed to the ministry of authority in the Church that they shall not only preach but also live the Gospel. These expectations are as real today as ever they were. People not only inside the Church but outside it believe rightly that in the way of life of an ordained minister they ought to be able to see a pattern which the Church commends.' Restrictions on how the clergy may behave stem from their pastoral function, it says, and 'as far as possible their lives must be free of anything which will make it difficult for others to have confidence in them as messengers, watchmen and stewards of the Lord.'

Meanwhile, the reality that countless clergy encounter is that when they put on a dog-collar, curious things begin to happen. At one level, they may become sexually attractive to others – whether this is because they act in a caring way towards someone whose own life lacks kindness or because they represent a powerful priestly figure at the Eucharist – while at another level, they become oddly neutered. The clergy spouse, meanwhile, is both the privileged individual who shares a bed with the 'holy' man or woman and also a potential rival for their time and attention. Within this context of contradictions, the priest and their partner have to negotiate their own marital and sexual relationship.

A number of clergy and their spouses confirmed this confusing experience. 'You're like the therapist, it's emotional transference,' Tom, a vicar, told me. 'You know, the "no one understands me like you do" syndrome. It's also because if anyone else in a traditionally vocational job, such as a doctor, gives someone their time, they're far more likely nowadays to say "That's OK, that's what I'm paid for", than the vicar, who'll say "That's what I'm here for". There's something very powerful in that.'

'It's the "otherness" that seems to appeal to people,' says another minister, Andrew. 'The fact that you've opted out of the rat race, and you're different, you have different values. That can be very attractive.'

'People in the parish react differently to him when I'm there,' says Pippa, a priest, married to a vicar, but working in a sector ministry herself. 'That's what really bugs me. It's as if they have some prior claim on him, or as if they think they know him better than I do.'

Another wife, Melanie, says, 'Whatever the appointment, a clergyman attracts a group of women who can be quite forward with him. These situations can normally be laughed at when the marriage is sound, but they can also be very stressful and dangerous when a marriage is going through a rough patch.'

The pitfalls of pastoral care are well-documented, and very real. The fact that the clergy spend time with people at times of great need and emotional turmoil, that their hours are unstructured and that their work involves their meeting people in private in their homes or clergy houses, calls for clergy to have a high degree of self-awareness and caution. Every year the tabloids seize on the latest scandal where a vicar is accused of adultery with one (or more) of his parishioners.

'You've always got to be careful,' said one of the clergy in *Revelations*. 'Clergymen are constantly tempted, just like anyone else. I mean, I know I'm a sexual creature, and for me to say I wouldn't be tempted just because (a) I'm very happily married and (b) I'm a clergyman, is just ridiculous: it would be denying my own weaknesses and denying my own sexuality, as well as denying the other person's . . . I'm always very, very careful about getting into one-to-ones with women, because of the kinds of relationship which can take place.'

In their detailed study of clergy marriage, Kirk and Leary claim that unresolved questions of sexuality are widespread among the clergy. 'Sexuality and gender figure largely in the problems clergy experience in their marriage and their ministry, though the issues may . . . be unrecognized or unacknowledged,' they write. Many clergy, they continue, are very unwilling to talk about sex, and if there is a problem, reluctant to seek help. 'We have a sexual problem that's been dragging on,' one clergy wife admitted to me. 'I think we probably need counselling, but I just can't face it. What if anyone in the parish found out, or if the counsellor discovered he was a vicar? I'd die of shame.' Another said, 'Sex? What a joke.

We used to have a good sex life, but that's a folk memory now. Working the hours he does, he's always too tired or stressed out.'

Deep down, perhaps, many of us are still stuck on the idea that the body and soul are somehow separate, and that the physical does not merit the attention the spiritual requires. As Christians, the clergy and their spouses may be too busy fighting the desires of the flesh, and focusing on the things above, to take an honest look at some of the thornier questions raised by our needs as human beings. But if we accept that life in ministry can be pressurized, it soon becomes apparent that if there are any cracks in a relationship, they need to be attended to. It then becomes little more than common sense to develop a high degree of self-awareness where our sexuality is concerned.

PUBLIC PROPERTY

'You are not simply a married couple. People feel that you "belong" to them,' said one wife, Alice, when I asked if there were any stresses specific to clergy marriages. 'Your business is everyone's business. Your time is never exclusively your own unless you are away from the parish. You are expected always to be smiling and happy. Privacy becomes a rare commodity. Intrusions into your private life are considered to be acceptable. Your home is not your own but an "extension" of the church hall . . . I could go on.'

'Everyone knows who you are, and where you live,' says Carol. 'Being a public figure, always carefully observed and commented on, can be a terrible strain.' 'The lack of privacy is an enormous problem,' says Becky. 'In what other job is there such a close overlap between home and work? It's things like not being able to take a holiday at home or finding if you sit down together and open a bottle of wine someone calls or getting fed up with a fussy mum at school, who also happens to be the church treasurer. It's invasion by anything or anyone at any time.'

The irony of the 'goldfish bowl' scenario is the fact that it is generally a one-way process: many spouses reported that concerns about confidentiality or loyalty frequently stopped them sharing their own difficulties and frustrations with those same people.'You can't really share too many problems with parishioners, such as struggles in your marriage or problems with other clergy,' says Harriet. 'You have to have an outlet outside the job or you wouldn't survive.'

Another wife says it is the expectations people have of her that are most stressful. 'It's the extent to which the clergy wife is asked to participate in her husband's vocation,' says Catherine. 'Even those wives who have their own careers are subject to the entrenched expectation that they will be active members of their husband's church and active supporters of their husband's work. The understandable resentment that some wives feel at being seen as an extension of their husbands, and the struggles they face in negotiating a separate identity can produce severe tensions.'

Many of those who took part in my survey had at some stage encountered the assumption that clergy marriages should be perfect. 'Oh yes,' says Katie. 'Most people here would think we had the perfect marriage and that we're holed up in the house praying and oozing joy. People *expect* us to have the answers, expect us to be sinless.' 'Everyone else can have marriage problems, but you must be all right,' says Mary.'If there is any difficulty, you have to be seen to be working things out, it's a public responsibility.'

'I am wary about letting Nick down by being annoyed with him in public or revealing a lack of communication between us,' says Sally. 'But I've discussed this with my mother, who is also a clergy wife, and we both think this is more to do with protecting marital privacy, rather than with trying to pretend everything's always perfect.'

'I think people are a bit more realistic these days,' says Sheila, whose husband is nearing retirement. 'It was a great pressure in the early days when we were first married. The thing is, that sort of attitude actually puts great stress on a marriage, if you end up having to appear in public very differently to the way you feel inside.'

For many, this is a source of annoyance. 'Surprisingly, we've experienced that kind of expectation from the family,' says Jeanette. 'People imagine us to have a serene and peaceful life with little stress. We are at home together all day (ha, ha) in our quaint little life. We are seen as some kind of ideal couple who live in a perfect world unaffected by real life. We are burdened with family problems, as if we have a magic answer for everything, as we have the "perfect marriage". We are seen as never having any problems, while the rest of the family have their very normal ups and downs.'

A number of spouses testified to making a conscious effort to make people realize they were no different from anyone else. 'I do try to indicate that we are an ordinary couple by referring occasionally to things like family worries, our differences, tiffs, problems with teenage children and so on,' says Katie. 'Parishioners are astounded when I relate arguments that Henry and I have,' says Louise. 'They think we never argue. Henry hates it when I tell people, but I think they need to know that we're real people.' 'We make it clear that we are human and fallible,' says Rhiannon. 'And if we don't, the children do it for us!'

One or two reported meeting not only public expectations, but also resentment from others. 'There is this assumption among Christians, heightened in the case of the clergy, that if you marry a Christian, it will all be OK. Friends with non-Christian partners can be very resentful. As it is, we are a very close couple, but sadly I don't think this is the case for all the clergy,' says Becky.

'There's this "it's all right for you" attitude,' says Anne. 'When our son was dangerously ill with meningitis, a number of people prayed for him, but one or two were almost cross when he recovered, and others they'd prayed for didn't.' 'This week a lady whose husband had left her and who was being evicted because he wasn't paying the mortgage said to me, "Of course *you* won't have that trouble with your husband",' says Jean.

Inevitably, it seems, at particular times in their lives, people project their own anger and expectations onto the clergy and their families, and it takes a certain amount of strength not to take such hostility or criticism personally. Many spouses, however, testified to a great deal of warmth and support from parishioners. 'People can see that Tom and I are very happily married, but I think they are pretty realistic anyway,' says Diana. 'Some do show real concern whenever there has been a particularly busy or stressful time in our lives and have been very supportive.'

'The early years of Richard's ministry put a great strain on our marriage, and if we had parted, some people may well have felt let down,' says Ruth. 'However, by far the majority of our congregations have always sympathized with the strains and stresses they believe a minister's life imposes on a marriage. He and I live fairly independent lives now, and although I'm sure this is noted and perhaps remarked on, I have never been made to feel that this arrangement is wrong.'

From my own experience, one of the most important things I've had to hang on to is that it can take only a single hurtful or negative comment from one person on a bad day to make you feel that the whole parish is conspiring against you. In fact, of course, for every critical or thoughtless voice you do hear, there will probably be at least another 20 people who are being quietly supportive, considerate and thoughtful.

In 1996, the newspapers reported that Canon Michael Green, a leading evangelical preacher and the Archbishops' Adviser for the Decade of Evangelism, and his wife Rosemary had had a spell of considerable difficulty and violence in their marriage during the 1980s. They subsequently received counselling, and Michael Green reportedly described their marriage as 'gloriously sorted out now'. What did emerge, however, was that, during the bad time, Michael Green's average working week as Rector of St Aldate's, Oxford, was 96 hours long, and included running a city-centre church, frequent student missions, prolific writing and personal ministry to many who came to him and his wife for help.

All the spouses I surveyed were agreed that the hours 'on duty' were very long, even for those clergy in less high-profile jobs than Michael Green's. Many cited the working hours as the most significant stress factor. One curate's wife, recently married, gave up her teaching job because she felt she could no longer cope. 'When you get married, you want to spend time with that person,' she says. 'I was working from 8 till 5, Monday to Friday, and then he was out every evening. It was terrible. In the end, it was a choice between his job or mine. I handed in my notice.'

Some wives who are at home full-time find it little easier. 'It's great for young children, to have a dad around at odd moments during the day, but as a wife you have very little time alone with your husband,' says Clare. 'It's all those endless evening meetings.' 'When Frank was a curate, he had a 7 a.m. Communion service every morning. That was crippling on us, as a family with young children,' says Sue. 'After endless broken nights, they were woken every morning when he left the house, and we never had a lie-in. And he always came home late at night. Hence two years of exhaustion and resentment on my part!'

Many described the pressures of the ministry on married life as being intense. 'The major negative effect is that John can hide behind his job, and not face what goes on in the household,' says Katie. 'The retreat to the study is a classic, and of course everyone else sees my husband as "super-spiritual".'

'Because the effects of parish life have been so hard – for both of us – we have been more vigilant than perhaps we otherwise would have been in tending to our marriage,' says Catherine. 'Knowing how easily the parish can overwhelm everything else in our lives, we are conscientious about spending time with one another. And because the church offers us so little support, we have worked very hard at supporting one another. So, on the whole, the stresses of my husband's job have had a strengthening effect on our marriage (though they have made my attachment to the C of E considerably more difficult). I should add that the absence of children in our marriage and the mature age at which I married (38) have made it easier for me than perhaps for many to cope with the stresses of a clergy marriage.'

'I married an army officer who had no intention of being ordained,' says Joanne. 'The pressures of that job were amply compensated by the privileges it brought. Now my husband is a vicar, but we have no concrete privileges that anywhere near compensate for the pressures he is under.'

'William's job has made our marriage seem like a constant struggle,' says Alice. 'Our faith is what has kept us together. I feel sure that if he had been in another job, we would have had more time to talk things through rather than issues taking months or even years to be resolved, because there is always something to do or somewhere else to be.'

From our own experience, we have learnt that committing ourselves to taking a proper day off together is absolutely crucial, and the one time that tensions do arise is if, for any reason, Ben's day off has been badly disrupted. If events intervene, and it does happen, we now make a very conscious effort to find another time, as soon as possible, to catch up with each other.

The majority of people I interviewed felt that having more time off together would be an enormously positive benefit, even where there were no specific difficulties in their marriage. 'Tom loves his job and is very fulfilled by it,' says Diana. 'And this has a very good effect on our marriage, producing a strong sense of who we are and where we are going in life. Paradoxically, this positive can turn into a negative if enthusiasm for the job is not balanced out by sufficient time with family and friends. Ten years' experience has helped us to achieve a better balance.'

Jo, at home with the children and devoting considerable time to parish work, says, 'David and I probably see more of each other than most couples, and we work well together, but it's very bitty. The fact that we are frequently exhausted and stressed means we have very little life outside the parish.'

'What I really find hard,' said Liz, 'is that Paul is always willing to give time to others when sometimes I need it.' 'Sometimes it's difficult to really "talk", because you're afraid of being another problem to weigh down your husband,' says Fiona. 'And although I see him on and off all day, I never really know when it's "my" time.'

Several people said that almost the only time they went out together was to social events within the parish. 'It's part of the job, but not a choice of relaxation, even when an event happens to be enjoyable,' says Melanie. 'There is then a real pressure on our time off together. There's a big danger of the parish pushing aside our marriage and family as a priority.'

Even on a day off, living in a vicarage can make it

difficult to relax.'We're often seriously taken for granted, and used as a telephone exchange or photocopying service,' says Linda.'And you can never take a week's holiday at home. Even with the answerphone, messages still have to be attended to. The only answer is to get right away but, financially, this is not always possible.' 'Living on the job is the biggest strain,' says Wendy. 'It's the constant interruptions to mealtimes, the phone ringing as you're putting the children to bed, days off when it feels rude to say to people that he isn't available, when he's standing next to me. And working at home, he finds it hard to switch off.'

A large number of the spouses felt that the content of the work of the clergy also contributed to the degree of stress experienced by the whole family. 'Jonathan's mother seems to have no idea about his job,' says Fiona. 'I remember one Christmas I was trying to explain that he was very, very tired, and she said, "Oh, I would have thought a job like his would be very energizing". She doesn't seem to have any idea how exhausting it is having to be *nice* to everyone the whole time.'

'The job is so all-consuming – there's so little separation between home and church and work – that there can be a lot of tensions,' says Felicity. 'Giving out to so many people can mean there is nothing left for the marriage. I think there's a great temptation for the clergy to neglect both their marriage and the self.'

It would be quite wrong to draw a picture of unrelenting gloom about the marriages of the clergy and their spouses. By focusing on some of the difficulties, and drawing out some of the experiences common to many, there is a danger of suggesting that anyone who marries a minister is doomed to misery. In fact, while most spouses found some aspects of the lifestyle of the ministry imposed a degree of stress on their marriages, many made it quite clear that they considered that the overall benefits outweighed any negative aspects.

'I feel that although much of the "sorting out" we have had to do (and continue to do) has been difficult, wearing and at times painful, the overall effect of his ministry on our marriage has been positive,' says one wife. 'In many ways I think it has strengthened our relationship. I remain optimistic that what we are both doing is trying to live out our ideals and develop an appropriate, holistic and celebratory lifestyle.'

'Seeing other people's marital struggles makes me very grateful for what we have,' says Clare. 'I can participate in his job more than other wives can, and I like that, although I'm sure some people wouldn't. Yes, there are demands, night and day sometimes, but it's wonderful to have him at home during the daytime, and I really love the fact that he does do quite a lot of work at home.'

'It's something we choose and do together on the whole,' Melanie told me. 'He is happy in his vocation, and therefore happier with me. Mostly, it has brought great fulfilment and purpose to our lives together.'

Many expressed their overall feeling about their marriage in terms of their Christian faith. As Felicity says, 'Our faith was central to our marriage and it still is. I feel deep down quite confident that we are in it together, even though I don't do anything high profile church-wise, and although at times I have felt neglected by the hierarchy.'

'We both have a faith which is fundamental to us and our lifestyle,' says Becky. 'I have always understood and respected that Keith was called into the Church. We pray together, and I frequently give him advice. Equally, Keith *never* takes my support for granted.' 'Our marriage relationship has become stronger and deeper over the years and especially since we became Christians 15 years ago,' says Harriet. 'Without our faith it would be extremely difficult to cope with the stress levels involved in clergy life.'

The point that emerges here is surely not that clergy

and their spouses always have to 'get it right' or have a perfect marriage, but that they should make absolutely sure that the marriage remains a priority. Anyone who has exchanged marriage vows has a clear duty to devote time and energy to each other, whatever the outside demands. Equally, for couples who are encountering difficulties, the mechanism for appropriate and completely confidential counselling needs to be in place, so that problems can be dealt with before they become too enormous to deal with. Frankly, marriage is too important to neglect.

4

FAMILY LIFE

In the late 1980s and early 1990s, a number of high-profile (male) politicians and cabinet ministers resigned from their posts, not because of any policy disagreement or scandal, we were assured, but because they wanted to spend more time with their families. 'Spending more time with the family' thus became a euphemism for departing under a cloud, for professional failure. The implication was that while real men stayed the course, those who couldn't keep up with the pace dropped out and scuttled home.

The idea that family life is somewhat second-rate in comparison with 'real' work has historically often prevailed among the clergy as well. The former bishop of London, Graham Leonard, illustrates this dilemma in *Revelations.* 'When I look back at the way I neglected the family . . . I feel really ashamed,' he says, reflecting on his years of ministry. 'I mean, it was partly out of sheer pastoral care for the parish, but it was also, I must admit, partly out of a desire to be thought of as a good parish priest. I can remember thinking, "If I go and help my wife in the garden, people will think I'm neglecting my job." ' In retrospect, he admits this was a mistake. 'Well, that was a totally wrong thing to think, but I did and do feel that I neglected the family in those years.'

Considerable tension arises from the fact that the better the priest appears to do the job – that is, the more available, caring and willing to give of themselves they are – the less the rest of the household is likely to experience these same qualities from the clergy parent or partner at home. Yet, at the same time, if the Church is trying to teach anything about so-called 'family values', concern for family life ought to be mirrored in the lives of its clergy.

The particular threads of concern about family life expressed by the spouses in my survey were the ever-present squeeze on time together, the difficulties of living in certain parishes, the pressures on bringing up a family in the public eye, and the expectations people have of clergy children.

QUALITY TIME

It is worth quoting at some length an account of the realities of vicarage life as described by Richard Harries, Bishop of Oxford, to Mary Loudon for *Revelations*: 'Vicarage life is a great strain on family life because there is no clear distinction between work and home. The particular strain is on the wife, because she's usually got her own career, plus the family, plus parish expectations, which means one more set of expectations on top of the normal two which most women find difficult enough to manage. I'm not sure that the clergy divorce any more than any other group, but there are certainly more clerical separations than there were, and it's not surprising. You've also got the particularly constraining situation of the vicarage itself, and the difficulty of getting time off when you're in it. You particularly notice it when you go away for a lovely holiday and the minute you walk in the front door you're back at work. The doorbell's going and the telephone's ringing because you're living over the shop.'

The solution, suggests Bishop Harries, lies in making a

conscious effort to redress the balance: 'You actually have to take positive steps to be able to manage work and marriage, and you have to believe that it's worth spending time with your family rather than time on Church meetings and parish business. You actually have to believe that's important and want to do it. Some clergy really are able to do that and I admire them. Most clergy overwork and find it difficult to manage that side of things.'

This is not something he has found it easy to do himself: 'I would say that I have a tendency to overwork,' he says. 'I really admire those clergy who are able to be that much more unpopular with their parishes because they give more time to their children or spouse or whatever, but I've found that difficult.'

In his account, Bishop Harries puts his finger on a number of points voiced again and again by the spouses in my survey. It is not just the working hours, but also the constant interruptions; it is not just the external demands of the parish, but also the tendency of the clergy to overwork; and getting it right requires a very conscious commitment.

The working hours of the clergy, as we have seen in Chapters 2 and 3, are long, and often antisocial, with the frequent evening meetings and weekend work, and at times they appear to militate against family life. 'The hours are difficult, especially when children are small (or large, for that matter) and need to see both their parents regularly,' says Sheila. 'Now that our daughters are grown up I feel we probably have a reasonable balance between work and home, but that was not so while they were younger.'

'More free time together with the children would be wonderful, but it's never easy to have time off at weekends or in the evenings', says Carol. 'A weekday off is no use now that the children are at school, although he's often around at tea-time,' says Jean.

A number of women felt that their husband's working

hours put a disproportionate burden on them to keep the family going. I have sometimes found my heart sinking during the run-up to major festivals, such as Easter and Christmas, when Ben is permanently busy, out or exhausted, and the children and I are on our own at the very times I would like us to be together and celebrating as a family. 'I sometimes think I'm married on my own,' says Marion. 'I often feel like a single parent,' agrees Joanne. 'My husband has *never* had enough time for the children, and that has always been an issue for us,' says Katie.

The frequent interruptions to family time and the lack of privacy can grate, too. I find it frustrating if the children have just come home from school and we're catching up on their day or reading together, and the phone or doorbell rings, yet again. Nowadays I tend to put the answerphone on. 'The children don't always like it, especially when groups come to the house,' says another mother, Vanessa. 'But actually we've chosen to do it that way, rather than having Don going out so much.' 'In our experience, older children and teenagers require privacy and their own space,' says Beth, a mother of four. 'We try to give them that, but it's not always easy in a busy house.'

A number of people said that they had worked out conscious steps they could take to help the situation. 'We tend to go away during school holidays and half-terms so that we have quality uninterrupted time with the children,' says Anne, whose husband was ordained when the children were in their teens. 'As they are now old enough to understand the situation, they are very supportive. We do explain some of the issues we are facing and try to stick to agreed timetables so that they know the score and don't feel left out or let down.'

'After a number of stressful years we have worked out a system that suits us,' says Ruth. 'However, if we had more than one child, I do not think I would be able to cope as well. I have enough time with my husband and enough time with my daughter, but I still do not feel we spend sufficient time all together.'

Sometimes parishioners can be less than sympathetic to the importance of their minister's family life. 'When we first came to this church, I was not always available to attend meetings, because of meeting the children from school,' says Sheila. 'On the night of our welcome here, in that context, one lady said to me, "We've always been very lucky here, as we've never had a minister with young children before." Now people say it has been great having children growing up in the manse.' 'Our attempts to put the children first are often received grudgingly,' says Julie. 'For instance, once when one of the boys was playing in a concert and Phil tried to change the time of a meeting, they were not very helpful.'

As Kirk and Leary noted in *Holy Matrimony?*, 'A parish wants the happy vicarage family with its 2.4 children, but it is often loath to accept the implications of this ideal.' A parish may want its priest to live out the ideal of Christian marriage, but also expects them to be infinitely and universally available.

On the other hand, as Felicity, a wife and mother commented to me, 'I wonder if some clergy families might take themselves too seriously, and set themselves apart by establishing barriers and distancing themselves from their community. Of course we struggle constantly to have quality time as a family and as a couple, but surely every family does this.'

The crucial aim, surely, is to ensure that family life remains a priority, whatever this means in practice. For us, on the afternoons that Ben collects the children from school and cooks our evening meal, he (or one of them, if he forgets) always takes off his dog-collar, to make it quite clear that this is their time. Another family I know always has tea together after school, when the answer-phone is switched on and the news of the day exchanged. A third family says that its sanity is saved by having a large dog which forces them out of the house together at least once a day.

DIFFICULT DECISIONS

The frequency of job moves, and the wide range of ministerial options, means that clergy families have to face the difficult question of where they are going to live at regular intervals. This brings to the surface all the tensions between a possible calling and the realities of day-to-day life for the rest of the family.

Uprooting a family and moving repeatedly is not by any means something that is unique to the clergy, but that does not lessen the strain it puts on the household. Indeed, moving house comes third on the list of highly stressful life events – death and divorce are first and second. Moving may, however, on occasion, be a source of excitement or perhaps a relief if the present parish is a difficult one, but it may also entail leaving other family members, friends, a school where children are happy, a spouse's job or a vital network of support. 'It's starting again that's the worst thing,' says Alistair, who has moved several times in the course of his wife's ministry. 'New place, new routines, new friends. It's back to square one each time for the whole family.'

Historically in the Church of England, the (male) priest was called by God – or sent by the bishop – to a parish, whether or not it suited the rest of his family, and there are still some in senior posts in the Church hierarchy today who support such an approach. But for the younger generation of clergy families, this is increasingly viewed as being unacceptable. Many spouses reported that, although on several occasions they had felt overlooked by the Church hierarchy, any decision about their future as a family would be a joint one.

One clergy wife wrote a letter to the *Church Times*, expressing why she felt that the decision process involved the whole family. To be on the receiving end of the appointments procedure was, she said, 'to feel like an insignificant and easily overlooked part of the jigsaw'. 'In our household we dealt with this by discussing and being very clear with ourselves about what would be acceptable in terms of location, housing and schooling, and what would not. We had to have these discussions early, so that we would know how to respond when the moment came. We brought to this discussion our knowledge of ourselves and our family, our strengths and our limitations. Some clergy households, like ours, will need to set their own boundaries, and this should be welcomed as active participation in the appointment process, not as a negative approach ... it is his calling, not mine, and I need to safeguard my interests and those of our children, I cannot expect the Church of England to take account of my needs unless there is some way of making these known.'

However, even the most equitable involvement in job-seeking does not dispatch with the types of dilemmas faced by the clergy family. 'For myself, I wouldn't mind where I was or what I was asked to do, but because I'm married with three small children, that's where the cutting edge starts to come in,' said one of the (female) clergy in *Revelations*. 'I mean, I don't feel my children should sacrifice, say, their education because of my vision of where I should be. On the other hand, we go to places as a family, and if other families are living in housing estates in the middle of Birmingham or the middle of Manchester, then why shouldn't we as well? Just because we're middle class, why shouldn't we be there with the marginalized? So far we've not had to resolve that contradiction – and there is a contradiction there ... I think you have to say to yourself, OK if other people are enduring violence, perhaps we, as a clergy family, might be able to do a little bit towards countering that. When you've got three small children it's a very very hard question, but if we have to face it we will.'

The realities are not to be underestimated. In the same book, another priest recalls life in one parish: 'People threw rocks and bricks through the front and back windows. My car was vandalized. My kids were beaten up. One churchwarden abused my children, verbally, physically, made their lives hell. The garage was busted into, the kids' bikes were stolen, we were fair game for anyone who wanted to have a go. We were like Christians in the lions' den, and it was lions 100, Christians nil.'

In the end, he looked for another job. 'My wife and family up to that time had done what I wanted to do. You know, if Dad wanted to do this, they followed, they didn't have a lot of choice. I suddenly realized that they were people too and whilst I'm prepared to put up with the garbage that this place throws at me, and maybe I'm robust enough to be able to do that, they may not be. I thought, stuff this. I had seen my children suffer, I had seen my wife suffer, and I had had enough . . . so I started to say to myself: actually, my wife and kids deserve better, and I think I deserve better.'

One of the spouses in my survey, Sue, who, until recently, has been living in the inner city with her husband and three sons, aged two, four and six, told me that they had also decided to move out. 'Living here between two main roads is terrible and I do not like being constantly on call. Two murders and two attempted murders in the local pub in the last two months are not reassuring. We have already sent the children to a small rural school, out of the city, and now we're moving out to a holiday cottage we bought nearby, to reduce stress. Frank will keep his job in the city, and have an office next to the church.'

Others would say that bringing up a family in the inner city has brought them huge benefits. During the debate on clergy safety after the 1996 murder of the Reverend Christopher Gray, an inner-city priest, one clergy wife wrote to the *Church Times*, 'I resent the implication that, as a clergy spouse, I do not have a calling to share the risk of living in the inner city. I believe in a God who calls families to ministry, each member having their own part to play. God does not call to such ministry lone individuals who drag their families along as fearful and resentful baggage. I and my two children have loved living here . . . Yes, we have had the burglaries, car crime, bricks through windows and aggressive callers at the door. But overall we have gained far more than we have ever lost . . . I maintain that the inner city is one of the best places in which to live and bring up a family.'

Another reader wrote to the paper, recalling his father's early, and very successful, inner-city parish ministry, which was followed by a series of country parishes after his own birth. 'I can only think that I was to blame. Perhaps [the inner city] was thought an unsuitable place to raise a family. Was that really a good enough reason to deprive [the inner city] of my father's qualities? And was it really in my best interest to be shielded from the real world as I grew up?'

The simplistic answer is that every parish has its own particular demands, and every family will have varying needs as well as different strengths and abilities to cope. But, as the last writer put it at the end of his letter, 'What a fearful dilemma faces those who feel impelled to go where the need is greatest, but also yearn for a family and desire the best for them.'

CHILDREN IN THE PUBLIC EYE

A Radio 4 programme assembled a group of adults who were all children of clergy to discuss their experiences of growing up. The presenter who introduced the programme opened up the discussion by asking whether or not it was a terrible strain having to be 'good' the whole time. The contributors soon broadened the discussion to include other pressures, such as the continual interruptions, never seeing their father, coming to a decision about their own faith, desperately wanting to be 'normal' and coping with their father's fan club.

Bringing up your children in the public eye seems to be something of an occupational hazard for the clergy and their partners, and is something which personally makes me very uncomfortable. Recently, our six-year-old son said, 'Daddy, I like you being the vicar, because everyone at school knows who I am and talks to me.' Being the school mascot may be quite fun now, but his obvious visibility fills me with, perhaps unnecessary, foreboding for the future.

'Living as we do in a village, I think this is my biggest single worry,' says Jo, a mother of two small boys. 'What I have found is that any problems my children experience, such as shyness or late development, is obliquely attributed to their being the Rector's sons – quite irrationally so. Their development is closely watched by all!'

'I don't think my children liked being the centre of attention when they were young,' says Linda, whose two daughters are in their teens. 'I feel that the expectations of them are more obvious than any expectations of me. I think quite a few people are hurt by, and do not understand, our elder daughter's decision to stop going to church. She does not fulfil people's expectations of an outgoing, cheerful, helpful "Christian girl", and I think may be compared unfavourably, by a few, with her younger sister.'

'They are expected to be at church, and at all children's activities, but out of sight and earshot in the house', says Anne. Another mother, Jeanette, told me, 'My children are 13, 9 and 3, and I felt very sorry for them at our last welcome evening. One made paper aeroplanes with the name cards, and another one fell off her chair at the beginning of a speech and was too embarrassed to come out from under the table. They really felt that everyone was watching them.'

All the parents who took part in my survey felt that their children's behaviour came under public scrutiny in one way or another. On the second Sunday in our current parish, a member of the congregation turned to me and said with great friendliness, 'Isn't it wonderful the way vicarage children are always so good in church, even when other children are running all over the place?' When, as the mother of two only very recently reformed bandits, I begged to disagree, he smiled at me rather sadly and said, 'Well our last vicar had five children, you know, and they were always *beautifully* behaved.'

'In a parish, your children are under pressure to behave better than would normally be expected, just because everybody notices them,' says Alice. 'People make a big issue out of things that probably wouldn't be highlighted in any other lively child. My eldest son is starting school in September, and I have deliberately not said what his Dad's job is, so that he gets a fair start like all the other children.''There are certainly people in the Church who make a meal out of it if my daughter misbehaves, and she's only two-and-a-half!' says Clare.

This public scrutiny can be particularly painful for teenagers. A clergy friend of ours recently told us a story about his son, who was walking home from school one day with a friend. 'You live very near that church,' said the friend. 'Yeah,' said the vicar's son. 'The last bloke who lived here used to be the vicar.' Not long ago I came across an advertisement in a national newspaper that drives the point home again, were it needed: 'Embarrassing Parents? Are you embarrassed your dad's a vicar or your mum's skirt is shorter than yours? If you are an embarrassing parent, or your life's being wrecked by one, please call [a BBC researcher].'

'Oh yes,' says Beth, a mother of teenagers. 'People

expect them always to be good and tidy and polite.' 'I started going out with my husband, a vicar's son, when he was 15 and so I have vivid memories of the expectations of behaviour made on him and his three brothers,' says Wendy. 'My fear is that people have not changed in 17 years. My hope is that my children will be free to be themselves.'

Such pressures cause considerable problems for some families. 'I have a 17-year-old daughter from my first marriage, who got pregnant whilst doing A levels,' says Katie. 'That caused quite a reaction! Also, my 15-year-old son has been a problem at school. His own behaviour has been quite appalling at times, but he has had lots of trouble from other kids when they discover what his father does for a living. I feel very sorry for my children. I never considered for a moment that they would have trouble later on when I married my husband.'

'I think many people still think that as children of clergy are brought up "surrounded by faith", somehow they will be holy,' says Harriet. 'They are expected to take a lead,' says Mary, a mother of four. 'Their standards of behaviour are observed by their peer group, as well as older people, and judgements are made.' Another dimension of this expectation is the idea that somehow a clergy child might be a 'good influence' on another, just because he or she is a vicar's son or daughter. In one parish, there was a mother who regularly used to plonk her very unruly son into the pew with me, on the grounds that he might behave better if he sat with my son (highly unlikely in my judgement). In another parish, I felt acutely uneasy when it became apparent that another mother had singled out our daughter as a 'suitable' friend for hers, purely because she felt there was a certain cachet about the vicarage.

'There *are* expectations put on clergy children, but usually by the parents themselves,' says Becky. 'There should not be any difference from other children being brought up in a Christian home – some rebel, some conform. The only problem is that clergy kids get more comments.'

A number of parents felt they themselves were guilty of imposing expectations on their children. 'It is inevitable, and we consciously fight against the temptation to criticize our children's behaviour on the grounds that it ruins the vicar's reputation,' says Emma, who has three teenagers. 'I'm conscious of being in the public eye,' says Liz, whose children are much younger. 'I expect them to behave.' 'I don't feel pressure from parishioners, but I put pressure on myself as an example to others,' admits Louise.

Decisions about the children are also subject to the public gaze. One vicar and his wife I know made themselves extraordinarily unpopular by not sending their son to the village school, and other families in my survey reported similar dilemmas. 'We decided to send our daughter to a private school, even though Nigel is a school governor here,' says another mother, Maria. 'I didn't want the parish to decide about her future. I wanted it to be us who made up our minds. No one has ever said anything, but I'm sure they are a bit disappointed.'

This can work another way. When we lived in London, a woman I barely knew tapped me on the shoulder in the middle of Holy Communion one Sunday morning, demanding to know whether it was true we had turned down a place for our son at a much-sought-after church school a mile-and-a-half away in a neighbouring parish in preference for the supposedly rougher school at the bottom of our road. 'What was wrong with Christchurch?' she wanted to know. Which was the better school, and where should she send her daughter? I was horrified to think that what I had imagined was a private decision, made for reasons specific to our child and our situation, was being hijacked and presumed to be the authoritative answer for hers.

Many parents told of conscious efforts they made to resist public pressure as far as their children were concerned. 'We are our own people,' says Becky, a mother of four. 'We're not the type of family to stand on ceremony, anyway, and I would never introduce myself or the kids as anything to do with the vicar.' 'I try very hard to forget about what other people think,' says Melanie, who also has four young children. 'I try to let them be themselves, and remember that I'm not responsible to other people's expectations, but only to God.'

BENEFITS

Many of those I surveyed were keen to emphasize the positive aspects of bringing up their children in the setting of ministry. Some said that as a family they had been welcomed with open arms wherever they had gone; others felt that their children had learnt to be sociable from an early age; one or two families had been given family holidays by generous members of the congregations that they could otherwise never have afforded.

'When I think of my university contemporaries, they all commute and probably never see their children, whereas I can take them to school every day, and be around at tea-time when it's busiest,' Tim, a vicar's son and now a vicar himself, told me. 'And I have far more job security than many others, which is a great bonus.'

'Yes, it's rather public, but most folk have been very caring towards our family,' says Sheila, whose children are now adults. 'On the whole, our children have benefited greatly from being part of our Church family.' 'Our congregation all take a great interest in our daughter, and a significant number have really taken her into their hearts. I hope she will always be able to experience this extended family,' says Ruth. 'People always say how awful it is for the children,' another adult clergy child, Kate, told me. 'But I don't agree at all. You learn to get on with all sorts of different people, from all walks of life. I think it was a wonderful childhood.'

'I confess to being quite angry at times at the Church's alleged concern for family values when it shows such poor consideration for clergy families,' Catherine, a clergy wife, told me. Many of those I spoke to echoed this complaint: the pressures of the ministry are great, they said, and the demands placed on the clergy are not always balanced with support for the families supporting the priest.

In 1996, the Archbishop of York called on the clergy to make greater sacrifices in the sorts of jobs they accepted, which caused an avalanche of reaction. One came from a priest who wrote to the *Church Times*, 'I am not opposed to the language of sacrifice. Too often, however, it is used as a cover for the effects of mismanagement and pastoral insensitivity. Stipendiary ministers give up a great deal in terms of income and free time. But are they called to sacrifice marriages and health as well? We cannot afford such wastefulness . . . Those of us who are married may have our spouse's job to consider. We must also be aware of the effects of our calling on our children, if we have them. Having grown up in a vicarage, I regret the lack of time my father had to spend with me. Too many vicarage children are put off Christianity for life. We celebrate a full, perfect and sufficient sacrifice. Let's not try to outdo it.'

If we are living out the Gospel, we bear a responsibility to challenge such 'mismanagement' and give a high priority to family life, even where that means making painful changes in our approach. The clergy need to be conscious of the models of parenthood they want to present to the rest of the world. Family life is a messy business, in that it spills well beyond the home, and it may sometimes be difficult to set boundaries between private and public life. But the flexibility of the job, and the fact that they work from home, means that the clergy can be involved in family life, in schools, activities and friendships, in ways that other parents can never hope to be. The fact that other jobs are demanding and that other families also struggle to spend 'quality time' together does not lessen the commitment we need to make to getting it right. Settling for second best may otherwise prove too high a price to pay.

5

FAITH

Personal faith, and a call to serve God in the ordained ministry, is what gave the priest his or her vocation. It is not something that can be shed at the end of a working day. In the words of Kirk and Leary, 'God, and the living out of his call, intrude largely on the life of a clergyman and his spouse. Most clergy would claim that God in some shape or form plays a large part in their domestic as well as their professional life.'

Although for the majority of spouses a shared faith will typically lie at the heart of their marriage, it cannot be assumed that this will be automatically so, or that the relationship between faith, marriage and ministry will be totally untroubled. For many, a shared sense of vocation, lived out in partnership, may bring great purpose and fulfilment, but the whole business of God and Church, when interwoven with marriage, domestic and professional life, can also be a source of tension and resentment.

A SHARED FAITH?

Studies have shown that a good prayer life contributes directly and indirectly to the overall health of both the clergy and their spouses, yet Kirk and Leary's research found that the majority of clergy and spouses did not pray or study scripture together as husband and wife. 'God, who plays such a large part in shaping and structuring their daily round, is thus often excluded from the times husband and wife share alone together,' they write.

In my own survey, almost without exception, the spouses said they shared their partner's faith, although a number qualified this with comments such as, 'but I'm probably more doubtful and questioning' and 'we are in different places theologically'. One or two said they were 'not really' Christians, and a significant number felt that their faith had been considerably challenged in the course of their partner's ministry.

'Sometimes – most of the time, in fact – I share his faith, but it's difficult for both of us when I have a disbelieving moment, or day, or week,' says Liz. 'You need to know how to cope when your spouse spends their whole life working for God, and you feel totally inadequate, hardly giving God a thought.'

Another wife, Marion, says, 'It's still expected that a clergy wife is very devout and has a very strong faith. What do you do if you're like me and haven't? It's just another thing that gets in the way, an extra bit of pressure you can do without.' 'I know I don't do enough Bible study or have enough prayer time, and I wonder if, subconsciously, I'm kicking against the system,' says Karen. 'On the other hand, I feel my faith is well rooted by the solid continuity and purpose of our lives.'

One wife, Charlotte, recounted her experience when her husband was a curate and she went to a different church for some months. 'I was at a different place spiritually, and I didn't feel comfortable in his church. I know my husband found that very difficult, because he saw it as unsupportive, but at the time it was necessary for my own survival.'

Many people felt that being married to a minister and not having a Christian faith would be extremely hard. 'When, many years ago, I didn't share his faith, it made things very difficult for all of us,' says Marjorie. 'But he has shown me the way. He is a very humble person who plods on with God through thick and thin.'

'I honestly think that without our faith it would be impossible to cope with the stress levels involved in clergy life,' comments Harriet. Janet, a curate's wife, says,'I think the most miserable situation of all must be for the clergy wife who has no personal faith. It is an incredibly stressful and demanding job with little or no encouragement from other people most of the time. To have no vision for gospel work would make it all unbearably futile.'

STRUGGLES

No Christian could realistically expect to live life without having their faith tested. A number of the spouses I talked to, however, attributed particular spiritual struggles to the fact that they were married to a priest. Broadly speaking, the common threads that emerged were the effects of the day-to-day realities of parish life; the neglect of their own spirituality and the difficulty of their parish priest being their partner; and the idea that they were in competition with God for their partner's time.

'The trouble is that God and Church is"the job",' says Jo. 'So on a day off or holiday, you find yourself turning your back on it all.' 'The trivia attached to Church life gets me down, and sometimes makes me wonder whether it is all worth while,' says Julie. 'The nature of the job is such that one becomes aware of so many sad things and problems that it can be quite depressing at times', says Diana. 'It's spiritual pressure,' says Anne. 'Our heads are above the parapet. So we do come under spiritual attack, perhaps more than closet Christians.'

Others found the Church as an institution hard to cope with. 'Occasionally I've felt antagonistic to the Church and, by association, I've felt the desire to turn away from faith,' comments Wendy. 'The negative impact of my husband's job has not been my faith *per se,* but my relationship to the institutional Church,' says Catherine. 'What I have seen of the Church from the vantage of an "insider" has been deeply disillusioning, and nothing more so than its indifferent treatment of the clergy. I find myself having to struggle quite hard at times against a cynical and embittered attitude towards the church hierarchy.' Another wife, Joanne, told me, 'I've had endless crises over our financial situation, and God's provision. I keep feeling, Why me, Lord? Then sometimes I'm really proud that I'm married to "God's man".'

A number of people expressed difficulty with developing their own spirituality. 'I am the one person in the parish who has no priest,' wrote one clergy wife in *Married to the Church?* 'My husband cannot be a priest to me – our relationship is far too intimate. Who do I turn to when my faith is crumbling? Who is available to teach me and enable me to grow as a Christian? . . . Because I have no priest, I have become Church-dominated rather than faith-dominated.'

Some of the spouses in my survey expressed a reluctance to seek spiritual help from their partners for other reasons. 'I wouldn't want to be yet another problem for Jonathan,' says Fiona. 'If I was having difficulties, telling him might be adding to his burden,' agrees Liz. 'This does concern me,' says Sandra, 'but I have a friend who goes to a different church, who I know is there if I need to collapse.' Several spouses had turned to outside support, and a number had addressed the problem by finding a spiritual director.

'When Tom was ordained, initially I felt my spirituality was no longer important,' Diana told me. '*He* was the priest, so I felt God should work through him now. It took time to work this through. I know now that God speaks to me in a very different way, and that I often see things from a different angle, which is helpful. I've learnt to speak up and develop my own ministry.'

'I feel restricted by my husband being the vicar,' says Katie. 'I am a committed Christian, but I find it makes it hard to get close to people. I would prefer to worship elsewhere sometimes.' 'It can be difficult at times,' agrees Mary. 'I'm going through a stage of wanting to rethink the expression of my faith, both personal and corporate, and I find it hard to know how to do so in my own church, because of loyalty to my husband, and not wanting to interfere in his work.'

Some spouses expressed a sense of resentment of God, because of the demands faith in him put on their partner. Linda told me, 'My biggest fear is that in 30 years' time I'll *still* feel guilty for feeling that I'm in competition with God. I mean, I feel resentful of Oliver spending more time with other people who need help. He may be doing what God wants, but I feel bad, because I want more of his time for me and the children.'

Kirk and Leary found that this was a very common, although often unacknowledged, source of tension. 'Christian faith and upbringing can make it hard to rail at God. It is particularly difficult for a woman whose spouse has offered his life to God in response to a call, for what greater vocation can there be? ... If times of ministry conflict with family times, it way be well nigh impossible for members of the family to construct arguments of sufficient moral weight to achieve their husband's/father's time and attention, for they could be seen as standing against the demands of the parish, the Church, and, thus, God.' God can therefore very easily become 'the unseen enemy' or even 'the other woman (man)'.

Although painful, and threatening, such feelings are better admitted to and explored by means of discussion, prayer or counselling. Otherwise, the long-term effect will be far more damaging, both to the individual's relationship with God and with their spouse. As Kirk and Leary's study showed, if this anger remains unacknowledged, it will be internalized, and this can easily lead to depression, illness and despair.

FELLOWSHIP

'Just think of all those lovely Christian people you'll meet,' gushed a friend when she heard I was going to marry an ordinand. Of course she was right, up to a point: it is a great privilege to be part of a family that meets an immediate welcome into the heart of a church. In theory, a clergy spouse is uniquely placed to find fellowship, and many of those I talked to felt very comfortable within their churches. Others had met with difficulty or awkwardness, and some felt spiritually isolated.

'We are particularly fortunate in our present situation, as we share fellowship and friendship with our church-wardens and their partners,' says Harriet. 'I feel this is a real gift from God and quite precious.' 'I pray with one or two people about Church and personal things, and I pray with my husband,' says Becky. Janet says, 'Yes, I've found fellowship. There are lots of women in their thirties like me, some with children, too, and a few of us meet to study the Bible and pray, which is very encouraging. House groups here have been good, too.'

Pauline, a former Roman Catholic now married to a Methodist minister, comments, 'I have found that one of the greatest joys of the Methodist Church is its strong fellowship. There is a welcome for all, and various paths along which to travel – Bible groups, ladies' groups and so on. There is a genuine concern for one another's lives.' 'I have a spiritual director, and friends who pray for me,' says Felicity. 'I don't really expect to find a form of worship in the parish that will always suit me, though I don't close myself to unexpected pleasure, meetings and a sense of holiness.'

Others felt they were under certain constraints. 'I have been fortunate in both parishes to find one or two friends who I've been able to be honest with,' says Julie, 'but fellowship in larger groups is much more difficult because I feel I have to be careful what I say.' 'When I was in a small prayer group it was sometimes difficult, both ways,' says Sue. 'It was hard for the others, when they wanted to talk about their experiences in the Church, positive or negative, and for me when I wanted to talk about problems of faith or our domestic situation. So I have stopped going.'

'Generally, I've liked people in our congregations, but church fellowship as such has never been particularly important to me,' says Beth. 'I feel I need to be careful when expressing myself in a parish group, but I've usually found people I can express myself more freely with.' 'There isn't really much fellowship in this parish,' says Melanie. 'I feel that we should be building this into the groups we have by sharing openly, but I have at times felt too vulnerable to do that myself.'

'It's never been possible for me to be completely open in friendships within my church,' says Susan. 'Most of my "real" friends are in other denominations, or in previous churches – that is, they've developed after we'd moved on. I would have liked to have found the right clergy wives groups. Those I have attended have been somewhat suffocating.'

A number of people commented on the logistical difficulties in getting to events or meetings. 'It's been difficult attending evening fellowship groups when my husband is never able to babysit,' says Caroline, who has small children. 'Benedict gets so many more opportunities for nurturing his spirituality than I ever do.' Alice, who also has a young family, says, 'It's been hard work finding fellowship, but I feel this is largely due to my commitment to looking after the children which has "disabled" me in many ways. Finding fellowship takes time in my situation. I find this can make me feel quite lonely, particularly as William's experience is quite the opposite.'

For others, the problem has sprung from being in a church that has a tradition very different from their own. 'The people in this parish are not really from my background, or share my theology,' says Charlotte. 'It was very hard when James was a curate,' says Clare. 'The church was very traditional, and I didn't feel free to talk about God and my faith in the way I had been used to. I also felt squashed and rather disapproved of by our vicar's wife, and I found it hard to grow there spiritually.' 'I hadn't expected that I would find going to church such an alienating experience, particularly as everyone in the congregation is so welcoming,' says Lucy, whose husband has recently become a curate. 'In church I feel I only exist in relation to him.'

Others have found support from fellow clergy or their spouses. 'We've only just moved, but it's looking hopeful,' says Diana. 'Our church is a plant, so the congregation are mostly very young Christians, but we have a great staff team and as wives we get together, so there's always someone to share things with.'

Several people said that they had found fellowship outside their own churches. 'I never expected to find fellowship here,' says Christine. 'However, we can feel guilty when we go elsewhere to receive fellowship.' 'What you really need is to have some close friends in the area who you can really talk to,' says Marjorie. 'For five years we had another married couple we prayed and talked with, and it was marvellous support for us both.'

GOING TO CHURCH

'After more than 20 years of marriage, the big issue for me is still going to church,' says Marion. 'I feel I've got to be there, and I resent this. The children can make choices about whether they go or not, but if I don't go, it undermines his position. He is very dependent on my support.'

'There's great pressure on me to attend all four Sunday services. Sometimes I get overdosed on religion, if there are too many services and discussion groups and so on, and then I have to take time off to rediscover my faith,' says Sally. 'I would love to be *sure* that I went to church because I wanted to (as used to be the case) and not because it is expected of me.'

Being seen to be in church, week in, week out, is a pressure a number of people mentioned. They felt they couldn't have an off day, or even just a Sunday-morning lie-in, without attracting comment. When Ben was a curate, I had a very difficult few years, struggling with our babies in a church where there were only two other children who regularly came to church, both of whom were considerably quieter than ours and who also had the advantage of two parents to entertain them during the service. One man, a stalwart of the congregation, used to turn round and glare at me every week, and at the end of each service, would award me marks out of ten for the performance we had put up. It was torture. I felt I had to be there, both because it was my one chance to participate in worship, and also because we believed that children should be welcome in church. I also wanted to support Ben. Finally, when I was very sick with a pregnancy, and struggling unsuccessfully to keep a very determined and noisy toddler in the pew with me, a wise friend firmly told me to stop coming to church for a few weeks. I took her advice, and it was a huge relief, but the experience left me feeling angry and isolated.

Many other mothers echoed this sort of struggle. 'It's difficult to worship when you've always got young children with you,' says Jean, 'and impossible to get to services without them when you can't take it in turns with your partner.' 'I know there are other mothers whose husbands don't come to church, but I resent the fact that

I always have to take the children to services without his help, and that I'm on show,' says Liz. 'My problem is that I run a crèche for the children, so I miss out on worship altogether,' says Jo. 'If my husband wasn't the vicar, we'd take it in turns or I could go to an evening service on my own.'

GROWTH

Very many of those in my survey testified to the positive gains that their partner's ministry had brought them. Those who had struggled felt there had, none the less, been benefits. 'I feel I have a stronger faith now than I did five years ago,' says Caroline. 'I have leant on God a lot through some difficult times, and although I would not have chosen those experiences, the result has been a positive one for my faith.'

'The stressful times – which lead to all kinds of resentments and despair – in the end have forced me to rely on Jesus more and to pray more. I think Richard's ministry has made me struggle on when the going was tough,' says Ruth. Another wife, Marjorie, says, 'Because of his calling, I've probably endured more, and yet I've also experienced God's love more strongly.'

Many felt they had learnt directly from their partner's ministry. 'My husband's ministry has positively affected my faith in two fundamental ways,' says Catherine. 'I have drawn upon his often deeper theological understanding to enrich my own. And I have drawn faith from faithful people whom I would never have known were it not for their connection with him.' 'I'm sure his ministry has had a positive effect on my faith,' says June. 'There are times when Chris feels negative about his ability, and I find myself praying him through his ministry. In the past I often felt useless, but I've come to understand that nothing is more important than prayer.'

'I've learnt much and grown over the years in faith

91

from him,' says Melanie. 'I still enjoy and learn from his sermons and thoughts and opinions.' 'I've become less dogmatic and more thoughtful, and maybe more balanced in my outlook,' says Charlotte. 'I learn from his sermons and respect his ministry enormously.'

There were other gains as well. 'It has made me very aware of the privilege of working so closely with people at major times in their lives,' says Jean. Sandra agrees: 'It's had a positive effect on my faith because I am more aware of other people's difficulties and the way they deal with them, through his contacts.'

'I'm sure my relationship with God has grown deeper because of our full-time involvement in ministry,' says Wendy. 'Being so closely involved with what God is doing on a wider scale has helped me carry on when personally things have been a bit bleak.'

For any of us who are trying to live a Christian life, it is all too easy to let the demands of everyday life obscure our vision of God and hinder our faith journey. Within any Christian marriage, faith needs to be on the agenda. Even if husband and wife are in different places theologically, openness to each other's spirituality, and sensitivity to how that feeds into the marriage, is vital.

Clergy households are not unique in this, of course. What does become clear, however, is that there are a number of potential obstacles for clergy spouses, which need to be identified before they can be tackled. Whether the answer will lie in seeking a spiritual director, setting up a crèche in church or getting a regular babysitter in order to attend an evening meeting, going on a retreat or finding a group or friendship beyond the parish where it is possible to be completely honest, it will be different for everyone. But perhaps the first step lies in self-awareness, and making a commitment to not letting the spiritual well run dry.

6

HOME AND MONEY

Of all the issues I raised with clergy spouses, the subjects of housing, and perhaps even more so, money, brought some of the strongest and most diverse responses. Some felt that their vicarages were a wonderful bonus, while others bemoaned the fact that they had little choice about their homes.'The stipend is way, way too low,'said one wife. 'My husband often works 16 hours a day, 6 days a week, but money is always an issue. How can five people live on so little? We are even buying shoes from jumble sales now.''Of course we have enough money,' said another wife, a mother of seven, who has never had a paid job herself. 'We cannot be like Jesus if we are financially secure.'

In our affluent Western society, material possessions are something that Christians are often uncomfortable about. As long as acute poverty exists, we will face thorny questions about our material aspirations and lifestyle. For the clergy, these issues are compounded by the fact that some will be trying to run old or large houses without the financial resources or servants a previous generation of clergy might once have had, and that while they may feel embarrassed by their relative wealth in one parish setting, they will be the poor relation in another. Some would view the fact that the great majority of parish priests are paid the same salary as entirely just and appropriate, while others argue passionately for a rising scale or for complete equity across the board, so that bishoprics and other senior appointments carry no material advantages over parish clergy. For some, tied housing and the freedom from a crippling mortgage is a godsend, while for others the strings attached to the provision of a house make it unbearable.

TIED PROPERTY

The benefits of living in a Church house can be enormous, and are greatly appreciated by many spouses.'We have a lovely family home, larger than average, which we enjoy sharing with our family, friends and the community,' says Wendy.'We have no burdensome mortgage, and we don't have to think about buying and selling every time we move,' says Julie.

The variations between clergy houses from parish to parish and diocese to diocese are enormous: there are still old, traditional vicarages to be found, new, purpose-built ones, imaginatively adapted ones and plenty of others in between. Many spouses are enthusiastic about their homes.'We live in a far nicer setting than we could ever have afforded otherwise,' says Melanie. 'I love this house and garden. I feel it was God's present to us.' 'We have a really super house – roomy, well-appointed and with many luxuries, such as a big garden,' agrees Jo.

For others, while the absence of a mortgage may be a considerable relief, a question mark hangs over the future. 'Tied housing is a mixed blessing,' says Sheila. 'You do begin to worry as you get older, not knowing where you are going to live when you retire.'

Some people find that no longer living in their own home takes some adjustment.'Ten years on, I feel very positive about living in a manse,' says Ruth.'In the early years I missed not having our own house, but neither of us is very practical, and I have to say it is pure joy not to have to worry about repairs and redecorating. It is still a bit of a lottery, though. We are due to move next summer, and I can't help wondering what the standard of our new home will be.'

'For us, there are a lot more minuses than pluses about clergy housing,' says Harriet. 'For the first 23 years of our marriage we lived in homes we owned and chose for ourselves, and were therefore suitable in size and facilities for our family. Our first curacy house was decidedly cramped with one open-plan living room, a small kitchen, three small bedrooms and no study! Our present house was in an awful state before we moved in. We had to use a substantial amount of our own savings to put it in good order.'

Some clergy families I know have experienced a situation where the accommodation they were being offered was inadequate for the needs of both job and family. Expressing this sort of concern does not always meet with sympathy from the Church hierarchy or the parish. Two couples recounted that when they voiced their reservations about the housing provided, they were told that, as clergy, they should be above such material concerns. 'When we arrived [from a post overseas] we discovered, contrary to what we had been led to believe, that we were expected to reside in a poorly maintained house that had not been constructed as a vicarage and was ill-suited to function as one,' one spouse told me. 'When we protested that the house was unsatisfactory, we were told by a diocesan representative that he could not understand why we were so concerned about the quality of our accommodation. "Surely it's the job that's important," he fumed, "and if a grotty house comes with it, well, that's tough luck." It was that indifference that persuaded us to turn down the job.' The other couple, offered a small flat with no study, met a similar response.

A number of spouses also pointed to the difficulty of

being dependent on others for the maintenance of their home. 'We have a lovely big house, but it's owned by the Church and not the diocese,' says Clare. 'I hate having to ask for things to be done, and then there having to be 50 committee meetings and inspections before anything is decided. I'd rather my husband was paid more and we could decorate and improve the house with our own money. Though I suppose it would be hard to plough in too much of your own money, knowing you have to leave it here.' 'You have no choice about your home,' says Diana. 'You have to wait for other people to decide what decorations or improvements can be made, and when.' 'In this diocese the maintenance standards for clergy housing are notoriously low, and it is often difficult or impossible to get needed repair work done on a vicarage,' says Julie.

We were once made to feel very uncomfortable when a churchwarden told us that the parish would undertake necessary repairs and redecorate throughout before we moved into a curate's house. 'You choose the colours, and let us know what needs doing,' he said. We accepted this offer gratefully, only to be told, after the work had been completed, how extremely expensive it had all been. This was very unfair: it put us on an awkward and apologetic footing when we arrived in the parish, and could easily have been avoided, had he given us a budget and made it clear that we would need to meet any shortfall.

Clergy housing is certainly 'tied'; there are strings attached. Many spouses expressed the feeling that their home was not really their own. 'I feel frowned upon when I complain about the houses we are given to make into our home,' says Alice. 'Certainly having a large house is marvellous, but a badly planned modern vicarage can make life difficult. The vicarage is thought of in the same way as the church hall, with everyone having equal rights within it. It is easily forgotten that it is our home and the contents are ours, and we have our own way of doing things. It is certainly difficult to educate parishioners without offending them, and yet they would not dream of acting in the same way in each other's homes.'

Others said they felt judged on the state of the house or the way they chose to use their space. Certainly it is odd when you move in to a vicarage to find a large number of people already intimate with it. 'I like your new bedroom carpet,' someone said to me when we moved in to our present vicarage. 'Though, personally, I would have chosen the room with the wash-basin as the master bedroom.' The authors of the report *Faith in the Countryside* noted another aspect of this experience. 'The garden is an important feature of the rural parsonage and may be regarded as the last vestige of the days when the clergyman would have kept his own livestock and made his income from the glebe. A number of rural clergy have testified to being judged by the state of the garden, an important feature of rural life,' they found. They continued, 'We suggest that prospective rural clergy should bear this in mind as another particular feature of rural ministry, and we commend the provisions of the parsonage guidelines that the garden should be easy to maintain.'

LIVING ON THE JOB

Since the Industrial Revolution, work and home have tended to be separate. In recent years, however, this tide has started to turn; in our expanding 'contract culture', more and more people now work from home.

A recent study found that, instead of enjoying greater freedom and lower levels of stress, many outworkers worked harder and longer hours than their office-based counterparts. This will have come as no surprise to the clergy and their families, for whom there is no getting away from the job. Unless great care is taken, the priest's ministry intrudes and invades every aspect of the household. For the clergy, not only is home where they do their work, but work (in the form of people) physically enters the domestic domain.

For many spouses, this is a stressful experience. 'The fact that their residence is also their husband's place of work and that it is open to the parish implicates even the most independent spouses in their husband's ministry,' Catherine told me. 'Life in a vicarage is life in the public domain, and the strain of having no assured place of refuge from the parish is immense. My chief discontent as a clergy spouse is that our domestic life is subject to so much intrusion. I am astonished that the Church does not recognize how hard it is to have one's domestic life continually exposed to interruption. Gone are the days when clergy families were somewhat buffered by spacious vicarages and a staff of servants; yet no notice seems to have been taken of this fact by the Church hierarchy.

'I dislike the chronic disturbance of peace and the loss of privacy that comes with living in a vicarage. I feel that our home should be a sanctuary from parish life, and thus dislike the open-door policy we must practise. I *mind* that our domestic life is so exposed to public scrutiny. I *mind* that this causes me to worry about keeping my home and person perpetually presentable. I *mind* that when my husband is entertaining visitors I must restrict myself to a certain part of the house and remain as quiet as possible. I *mind* that when at home I can never entirely relax because the possibility of a visitor is ever present.'

Janet Finch discusses this aspect of vicarage life in *Married to the Job?*. 'Wives of the clergy perhaps provide the most extreme example of a home being on view, since the use of their home in the course of their husband's work is not confined to a room designated as his study, but often extends to the use of the family sitting-room for meetings of all sorts ... Certainly there are other occupations in which the home is used for work-related gatherings, especially in the use of "official residences" of politicians and diplomats. But there one would not expect the ambassador's wife to have cleaned the house before the party's arrival, nor that any lapses in housekeeping standards would be automatically laid at her door, as would usually be the case for wives of the clergy, who are put in the position not only of having their home used as a public place but of feeling that they are held accountable for its appearance.'

The overwhelming majority of spouses felt their privacy was often or frequently invaded; those for whom privacy was not a problem seem to form a tiny minority. 'Meal-times, story-times or a special night in are constantly interrupted,' says Wendy. 'I feel that the downstairs of the house always has to be clean and tidy because of parishioners dropping in or meetings held in the house. Some nights I just wish I could curl up in front of the telly with a bar of chocolate instead of being pleasant to people coming for a meeting.'

'I find it very difficult if I come home after a day's work and I can't go into the kitchen or the sitting-room,' says James, a clergy husband. 'Also, in this vicarage, even if Jenny is in her study, I can hear what is being said, unless I'm playing the piano. Sometimes I feel homeless. But that's partly because I'm naturally an introvert, while Jenny is extrovert. Even if she were not ordained, she would always invite people into the home, because that is how she is.'

'Our open-door policy has had a helpful effect in building up our Church family, but it has undoubtedly been detrimental to our private life,' says Mary. 'In a vicarage, there's a real lack of uninvaded personal space, despite living in a large detached house,' says Karen. 'You have all sorts of people coming to the house, some with problems, sometimes when you least feel able to cope with them, and you feel you can't walk around in a dressing-gown, in case you bump into someone.' 'Just sometimes I'd like to lock and bar the gates to stop people wandering up the drive,' admits Fiona. 'I just want to shout "Go away!" in true Christian fashion!'

Others find that living next door to the church can lead to constant interruptions. 'People call in if they've forgotten to bring their keys or they want to hire the hall, read the meters or even use the loo. And, of course, everyone knows where to find us,' says Harriet. None the less, many people truly want to be welcoming and hospitable and so struggle with the difficulty of establishing workable boundaries. 'I've always enjoyed having people come to my home and offering hospitality, but since I've lived in a clergy house, I've felt a bit invaded by people,' says Jeanette. 'It seems a little like public property. Having said this, some people are very good and sensitive about it.'

Some families have been forced to take active steps to protect themselves. 'We have a garden gate which goes into the church car park, and in the end we had to put a bolt on it,' says Becky. 'Otherwise you find people in the garden or even the kitchen – not a good idea when sunbathing topless! We have also insisted on a personal phone line, nothing to do with the church number, but that has its problems – who do you give it to?'

One or two spouses I interviewed who did not live in clergy houses commented on the difference it made. 'I really like the fact that our house now is not a parish house,' says Sandra, the wife of a college chaplain. 'When we were in the parish, I freaked out when Andy told me he'd had a communion service in our sitting-room – I felt like I had no home, no private space.' 'Living in our own home really helps, as it is not seen as Church property,' says Anne, whose husband is an NSM. 'We invite people to our home and use it a great deal, but people are very appreciative and don't take it for granted the way they might in a vicarage.'

Some clergy houses are exposed in their location. 'I like having the house open, but I have no privacy,' says Katie. 'When I sit in the back garden, people are always peering over the fence to say hello. Well, they say hello when they see me there, but they're actually just having a nose.' 'I'm very grateful for having a lovely big house, but the down-side is that you are never off duty,' says Wendy. 'It really is like living in a goldfish bowl. For example, though my husband works mornings, afternoons and most evenings, if he sits out in the garden for an hour he feels that people will think that he lazes around all day. So he doesn't like to sit out or have meals outside.'

'I'm very lucky,' says Melanie. 'We live in a quiet part of a quiet village with a big garden and a nice house and no noisy neighbours. I don't mind being public and joining in with village events, as long as I have private space to retreat to. Privacy is very important to me. When we lived on a small housing estate, very publicly, I found it stressful to be so exposed.'

One of the constraints of living on the job is the difficulty of taking time off, both because the vicar may find it hard to switch off when he or she is still in the workplace and because people will continue to call at the door and telephone. As Susan puts it, 'Relaxing at home on a day off or trying to take a holiday at home is impossible. People don't like it if they can't get hold of you, and even with an answerphone, messages still have to be attended to. The only answer is to get right away but, financially, this is not always possible.'

'In this job, privacy is not much of a problem,' said Alice, whose husband is now a college chaplain. 'But in the parish we found that if we were at home there was little or no privacy in our times together. Our neighbour

101

seemed to know our every move. Rumours were spread about us by those within and outside the church community. We found that on Will's day off we left the house early in the morning and came home quite late so that we could spend time together.'

Another potential problem is the whole question of security. In recent years, many dioceses have been forced to undertake a major review of the way vicarages are built and secured: burglar alarms, security systems and panic buttons are installed as a matter of course in many areas of the country. The incidence of violent attack against the clergy has increased significantly in the last few years, and the debate on the safety of the clergy continues. After the murder of an inner-city priest in 1996, one clergy wife wrote to the *Church Times*, 'While much has been said about the safety of the clergy in recent weeks, nowhere have I read of any concern for the spouses of the clergy. Many clergy spouses must, like me, have to open the door frequently to unknown callers. I have had a man push his way past me into the house – a frightening experience . . . I do hope that [the House of Bishops] will spare a thought for the spouses who are often alone in the house when roadsters, drug addicts and mentally ill persons and others appear at the door requesting help.'

Many of the spouses I interviewed echoed the same concerns. 'I really do feel *unsafe* when my husband is away, and scared on my own here,' says Katie.'We've had a few callers for money and, with young children in the house, I feel threatened when my husband isn't here to deal with them.' 'The number of gentlemen of the road who come to our door is increasing,' says Susan. 'They can be intimidating, and I worry when my son is alone at home.'

It is clear that, for a number of families, living in a vicarage can be a source of strain at times. There is no doubt that some clergy houses function better than others, in terms of their design and layout, and also that there will be variations from parish to parish as to what other facilities are available and how much the vicarage will be used for meetings. Equally, different households will have different ideas about the degree to which they want to open their homes to the parish.

A number of spouses suggested (not a new idea) that doing away with the traditional vicarage would significantly alleviate the problem. 'I would much prefer that the Church provided offices for the clergy on Church premises and paid them at a level that would enable them to purchase their own homes,' says Diana. 'This would permit some choice in the location, size, design and condition of their housing, as well as helping them to build towards their retirement. Until the Church is willing to provide clergy with offices that are detached from their homes (and adequate secretarial support) the lack of domestic privacy will be an acute source of stress in many clergy marriages.'

There have also been calls for the clergy to commute into inner-city areas, in the interests of safety. It is argued that just as doctors and other professionals frequently live outside their patch, the clergy should do the same.

Awarding the clergy a degree of autonomy over their accommodation would help to delineate between public and private. And yet, of course, such a move has significant consequences for the entire basis on which the parish structure is founded: that communities, by and large, will have a priest living in their very heart. *Staying in the City*, the follow-up report to *Faith in the City*, published ten years later, in 1995, strongly argued for the clergy to stay in the roughest areas of Britain, for the very reason that all the other professionals had moved out. This is not in any way to underestimate the realities of living in the inner city. As one clergyman, the subject of a frenzied attack by a drug addict, which resulted in several broken bones, two eye operations and several months off work, told me, 'If as clergy we are sharing in the redemption of the world, we must not withdraw. It's only by being where we are needed that we can do any good.'

STIPENDS

The clergy, someone once said, are middle-class men living in upper-class houses on a working-class income. While this might no longer be completely accurate, there is still, for many, a perceived discrepancy between the demands of the job and the financial package that accompanies it. There is an understandable tradition of the virtue of poverty within Christianity, which can translate into a moral suspicion about earning money. As one of the clergy in *Revelations* put it, 'People think the clergy have it easy. We don't. The clergy live like amphibians, in air and water. We live with a foot in both camps, and it's difficult, it's damned difficult to live with one foot in this world and one foot in eternity. On a more basic level, I could have been earning three times what I'm earning now if I had stayed in the computer business. I have no house when I retire. We do not have carpets you have to wade through. We do not change our suite every two years and go on foreign holidays. I should like to be able to live like some of my parishioners, even those who have retired ... What I would really like to see is clergy having a decent wage, being able to support a mortgage, and every church providing office space and ... a multi-purpose room where you could hold meetings and stuff.'

The authors of *Faith in the Countryside* found many clergy experiencing just this kind of tension: 'At one level there is little difference between the situation faced by clergy families and that faced by many other families in the countryside. The higher cost of living and the shortage of services are common to all ... However, clergy families can be caught between two stools. On the one hand they probably enjoy a reasonably high standard of accommodation without the worries of maintenance, but on the other they face the limitations imposed by the lack of local services and protected by only a modest level of income. In addition, clergy families are often expected to live as their predecessors did when areas of responsibility were smaller and incomes were relatively better. The predicament can be characterized as a tension between high expectations and limited resources.'

They went on to suggest that the level of pay was an important factor not only in family life, but actually in the achievement of a satisfactory ministry. At present, the clergy are not paid a salary, but a 'stipend', representing a financial allowance that enables the priest to carry out his or her work. But what do we expect a stipend to provide? Assigning ultimate financial value to any job is impossible enough, but how do you begin to do that with a job that carries a remit as broad as 'the cure of souls'?

According to the definition of the Church of England's Central Stipends Authority, the stipend should be adequate to allow the priest (without any private means or a working partner) to do their job, without unnecessary anxiety about paying the bills, and to be able to enjoy modest comforts. But this is very vague: how do you define 'unnecessary anxiety' (what degree of anxiety is 'necessary'?) and what are 'modest comforts'? One person's necessity will be another's luxury.

The authors of *Faith in the Countryside* offer a good illustration of this. 'The suggestion that married rural clergy may need two cars has been met with derision in some quarters,' they wrote, 'but the fact remains that multiparish situations require mobility and the lack of transport may impose severe limitations.' For this reason, they claim, it is very difficult to find clergy for rural parishes once their children reach secondary school age. Another point they made was the position of non-working wives who help in the parish. 'The Commission would like to acknowledge the role played by many wives of parochial and senior clergy, as unpaid secretaries, receptionists and producers of refreshments. Many open their homes to meetings. We feel that this work should be acknowledged financially and recommend that each diocese reviews this aspect of ministry with the intention of paying up to £2,000 per annum to those wives who undertake these duties, with special emphasis on those who do not have other paid jobs.' *Faith in the Countryside* was published in 1990; I am not aware that anyone has taken this idea any further.

Many of the spouses I spoke to were happy in the main with the stipend, which currently stands at about £13,000 per annum. The poverty of the clergy is, after all, only relative. I know that when Ben was first ordained, his curate's pay seemed to us riches indeed after being extraordinarily poor when he was an ordinand, but then we had never had two incomes, neither of us had ever had highly paid jobs and we had no children at the time. Personally, I was also extremely grateful to be able to make choices when the children were born about whether or not to go back to work, how much work to do and so on, unlike many of my friends who are tied down by expensive mortgages and have no choice but to work.

Some spouses felt their financial situation was the result of active choice, a stepping back from 'worldly' expectations. 'I know that Charles could be earning much more in another job, but so far that has not been important to us,' says Melanie. 'It's certainly better than the aid sector, which we came from,' says Charlotte. 'We have to be careful with our spending, but not being extravagant in our desires helps.'

Several people said that the pay was all right, so long as they had additional income from a second salary or other source. 'We do have some financial help from the family, and we live reasonably comfortably,' says Jo. 'The diocese is excellent about the house and that sort of thing. One big issue facing us is the need for a new car, but then many families are in a similar position.'It could be higher, and it must be difficult for families where there is no additional income,' says Fiona. 'Money is not really an issue for us, but then I don't know how we'd manage without our extra income.' Siobhan, in her fifties, went so far as to describe the package as 'very comfortable'. 'Think of the house and the job security, and then compare it with the conditions my children's generation face,' she says.

'In our experience, we do manage, but we have a supportive diocese who are paying for our elder children's education, out of the inner city, and we've received grants for holidays, too,' says Rhiannon. 'Sometimes it's difficult – we can't always buy the quality of items we would like – but, on the whole, we are very content.' 'Compared to secular employment and the long hours, it's poorly paid, but there is the flexibility in the job, and having a home,' says Emma.

Many felt that if the stipend were any higher, it would undermine their partner's ministry. 'If we have everything we cannot minister to those who have not,' says Marjorie, the mother of a large family. 'We must know the same battles as the flock.' 'I think it's about right,' says Caroline. 'Any higher and there would be a huge gulf between us and many people we have to work with. If it were lower we would be constantly worried about money and how we would cope.' 'We live in an area of high unemployment and a lot of people live off benefits and we must appear to be very wealthy,' says Wendy. 'Fortunately, we have never been a dual-income family so we have never suffered a drop in income. We have always managed on the money, and before I was supplementing our income we had help from a charity for our annual holiday. We've never had to go without.'

For others, the stipend has been a source of constant

financial struggles. 'I feel a huge amount of resentment that Edward is no longer a "real man"; he doesn't earn enough to support his family,' says Joanne, the mother of two young children. 'We have no choice about where we live or the size of our house, so the everyday costs of living are far higher than we would choose. At present, we cannot afford to replace a single major item of furniture in our home. Grocery shopping is often the bare minimum, with cheapest goods available, and we can't afford even a modest holiday. A modest rise to £20,000 would solve a lot of discontent. This is not an excessive amount – it is only what a good teacher or nurse earns. Surely our men are worth that!'

'It's all wrong,' says Becky. 'Long hours are expected of bright, educated men and women. I know there are other rewards, but the money is ridiculous. The house is a small benefit but there's no security. We have been very fortunate as I have always earned something and both our families are very generous. At this church – middle-class suburbia – people are increasingly supportive.' 'It's fine for us at the moment,' says Sally, a solicitor. 'But I shall never be able to give up work if we have children because we'd never manage financially.'

Elizabeth, with a grown-up family, and approaching retirement from her full-time teaching job, believes strongly that the stipend is failing to meet its aim. 'If the stipend is meant to be an allowance, and not a wage, it needs to be sufficient to keep you going. As it is, it is unrealistic,' she says. 'We live in a five-bedroomed house with attics, and it costs me £25 just to have the windows cleaned, and £500 to have a bedroom decorated. We can't afford to replace carpets and curtains out of £13,000. People think it must be wonderful to live here. It *is* wonderful, but it's impractical, and we've had to take in students to keep it going. I feel I am having to prop up the Anglican Church by working. At our age, we should be putting something away for the future, but we can't.

We could just about pay the bills if we didn't have a holiday or replace anything. I think the Church needs to be more creative in its thinking; at the moment it's all wrong, and unbiblical. If a man is worthy of his hire, he should be respected and paid accordingly.'

Others found the transition from a previous, better-paid life hard. 'Alan earned £40,000, plus a car, plus a £24,000 bonus in his last year of normal work,' says Janet. 'All our friends tend to be in that bracket, unless they are clergy, and the temptation is to feel the difference terribly. We seem constantly overshadowed by the prospect of not quite being able to afford things. Having said that, something always turns up and we could budget much better. Our expectations are quite high, as many of us come from professional backgrounds. Relative to the general population it is reasonably good though.' 'It really is too low,' says Harriet. 'Without savings from our previous life, we would find it very difficult to make ends meet and help two of our sons through university. We are much more careful with our spending nowadays.'

Many felt that the stipend allowed them to get by, day-to-day, but did not allow any leeway for sudden needs. As Clare says, 'Holidays are difficult, as we have very little savings. We always seem to spend up to our limit, and we sometimes have to delay grocery shopping at the end of each month until the next pay cheque goes in. I suppose we get enough – but that's all.'

'Because a clergy stipend provides no surplus income, it places families under the constant anxiety of wondering what they will do when an unexpected and unavoidable expense arises,' says Catherine. 'The answer is usually to go into debt, which the Church loudly deplores, but seems unwilling to remedy. For example, when my husband's car finally became too hazardous to drive, we replaced it with a very modest second-hand car, purchased through the Church's interest-free car loan scheme, which has now been scrapped. The monthly repayments were a constant source of financial stress, as it always entailed cutting back on some other necessity. The continual financial worry and constraint can make life quite grim at times and provides a breeding ground for resentment, particularly in view of how much the Church asks of clergy and their families.' The financial hardship, she says, strongly influenced her husband's decision to leave the Church of England for a job in America. 'Perhaps the most alarming aspect of the low level of clergy pay is that it makes long-term saving virtually impossible. In view of the precariousness currently surrounding clergy pensions, the stipends seem dangerously inadequate,' she says.

One or two spouses expressed disquiet with the whole notion of stipends. 'I associate the notion of a stipend with priesthood in the mode of Traherne or Herbert,' says Vanessa. 'It doesn't sit comfortably with modern ideas about clergy professionalism and the spread of managerial attitudes.' 'I think we should get rid of the dependency culture of the stipend, and pay adult salaries for the job that is done,' says Sandra. 'I also think that, for the benefit of families, there shouldn't be a housing element in stipends, and that people should be helped to buy their own home.'

The divergence of strongly held opinions illustrates how very difficult it is to discuss the question of clergy pay rationally. There are definitely difficulties and contradictions. If the stipend is supposed to be an allowance, not a salary, should it not take account of whether or not there are any dependants or a second income in the household? If the clergy cannot choose their own homes, could we allow for the fact that some clergy houses cost significantly more to run than others? If some appointments – such as archdeacons, deans, provosts and bishops – are deemed to carry greater responsibility and therefore higher rates of pay, should not other parish jobs be similarly graded?

Passions run high on the subject of money, and families coming into the Church from different backgrounds have very different expectations and needs. Those clergy families struggling financially perhaps need more support and help in working out survival strategies. Perhaps training at theological college in money management, or even dealing with debts, would be useful. Meanwhile, the wider debate on what constitutes a 'reasonable' pay scale will doubtless continue.

PUBLIC SPENDING

When we moved into our present vicarage, someone in the village told us that when it had been a private house, there had been a swimming pool in the garden. 'I wonder what the diocese would say if we unearthed it?' I mused. 'I think I'll start digging.' Ben looked totally horrified. 'We couldn't,' he said. 'We just couldn't.' A year on, the swimming pool (if indeed it ever existed) remains undiscovered; we 'just couldn't' justify having a swimming pool in the vicarage garden, even if we wanted to. And yet, I found myself wondering, why not? We could spend a few thousand (supposing we had it) on, say, a second-hand car or even a caravan, without comment, but we couldn't possibly spend a similar amount on a swimming pool, because pools are associated with luxury and a flamboyant lifestyle.

Spending, like so much else in the life of the clergy, is in the public domain. What you do with your money is very visible. Once, a parishioner gave Ben a sum of money which the donor insisted was to be spent on the family over the summer holidays. We took the children to Legoland, and had a great day out. The next Sunday, Ben made a passing reference to our outing in his sermon (I confess I can't remember quite why). 'I wish we could take the kids to Legoland,' another mother said to me after the service, 'but there's no way we could afford it.' I felt awkward and embarrassed; I didn't want to go into detail about how we had come to go, and yet I found myself longing to justify it.

As the financial pressures on PCCs increases, and churches have to become more responsible for funding their clergy, the expectation of getting 'value for money' begins to creep in. In 1996, Volkswagen ran an advertising campaign that played on this nicely. A series of advertisements promoting the low price of the VW Polo featured fictitious letters from grateful customers. One appeared from 'the Reverend Michael Wells': 'Dear Volkswagen, I can't tell you how grateful I was to see your advertisement proclaiming the price of a Polo. Only £7,945. Ever since I purchased one, my flock has been eyeing me suspiciously when I hand round the collection plate. I think they're harbouring less than Christian thoughts about how I could afford such a splendid motor car. I intend to use your advertisement in my sermon next Sunday, the subject of which is "Doubting Thomas. Does he still exist today?"'

The clergy, then, and their families, are expected to live out the ideal of Christian simplicity, but also to fit in to every social circumstance, which can be difficult. We are not supposed to be extravagant, but then presumably we should not be too shabby either. This was brought home to me when, within a month of moving in to our present parish, we received invitations to tea in a council house, a black-tie dinner party at the Manor, and to all sorts of gatherings at a whole range of households in between.

Satisfaction, or otherwise, with clergy housing and pay appears to have been a significant factor in whether or not clergy spouses were generally happy with their situation. Relative wealth, and relative poverty, will no doubt always be tricky for Christians. Many older clergy will argue that today's clergy have no idea how much better off they are now than used to be the case, while many younger clergy, perhaps coming into the Church from well-paid secular jobs, and stretched ever more thinly over multiple parishes, will feel that they are poorly rewarded for the long hours and expertise they bring to the job.

One clergy wife, with four children, summed up the dilemma she felt as a Christian. 'Sometimes I think we live too comfortably, and should be more different in our lifestyle from those around us. We certainly used to live more simply. Now we live in a very affluent area and, though we live on far less than most people, of course we still have more than some. It's hard. If you are in the ministry and haven't enough money, I imagine you could feel very inadequate and angry and jealous. But I've never felt that, as God has always provided.'

7

SUPPORT SYSTEMS

Clergy families have the same needs for social and emotional support, friendship and enjoyment as anyone else; this should be obvious. Add to the equation the fact that the clergy and their families are more often than not surrounded by people and you might imagine you had a recipe for unequalled social opportunities. Indeed, for many families, moving into a parish means being welcomed into a ready-made community, and presents a privileged and immediate way of meeting people and making friends. For others, however, living in a vicarage can be an isolating and lonely experience, where all sorts of factors – such as questions of loyalty, confidentiality or perceived favouritism – appear to get in the way of building close friendships. Also, contrary to popular belief, the clergy are not immune to suffering the common problems faced by the rest of the population, ranging from illness, pressures of work and general family difficulties to marital breakdown.

ISOLATION

Several years ago, a clergy wife wrote in the *Church Times*, 'The relative lack of privacy may have its disadvantages, but loneliness – or at any rate physical loneliness

– is almost impossible to experience in a vicarage. This may mean that clergy families may be unable to appreciate just how terrible loneliness can be, or how prevalent it is in the modern world . . . They live at the hub of the wheel: they know some of the anxieties, the hurts, the fears and failures of so many parishioners. If they are prepared to share them, they find great mutual comfort and love in belonging to that extended family of the Church.'

However, many of the spouses I interviewed reported that they did feel lonely and were struggling to make friends. 'It's a problem for us both,' says Linda. 'I have several friends as a mum through the children, but we find we can't really share with folks in the parish at a personal friendship level. One of the problems is that we're always too busy.' 'I was desperately lonely when Frank was a curate,' says Sue. 'It was terrible for about three months, until I began my own work and made friends independently from his job. I was miserable, and could easily understand alcoholism and depression in clergy wives.' 'It's lonely in that you don't make really deep friendships,' says Christine. 'Of course I know lots of people, but that's not the same.'

The reasons for this loneliness seem to be manifold, and will clearly apply in different ways to different people and situations. Some talked about the sheer pressure on spare time, which makes it difficult to develop new relationships or nurture old ones, and others of the need always to appear to be coping, of the problems of moving to a parish job a long way from family and old friends, and of the social isolation having the clergy 'label' brings. 'Theological college was a close community,' says Charlotte, a curate's wife. 'In the parish, though, you don't necessarily come across the same sort of person, with similar aims or desires or background to share experiences with. They keep you at a distance, not knowing what to expect. That's lonely at times.' 'People are friendly, but I wouldn't say we have made friends,' says Fiona. 'I am so grateful for old friends and especially clergy friends who know what it's like.' 'Yes, I'm lonely,' says Julie. 'It is very difficult to find people of my own age within the Church community. Also, Phil is so busy, and then so tired when I see him, that it sometimes feels as if I only ever speak to the children.'

For some, the clergy identity creates a barrier. 'If I'm honest, I've often felt alone, undervalued and only visible as "the vicar's wife",' says Felicity. It can be very hurtful to be treated differently, or rejected purely because of your partner's job. One of the clergy in *Revelations* recounted his wife's experience in his former parish: 'The congregation has treated my wife abysmally,' he said. 'For instance: if the plumber comes and does a job at your house and makes a cock-up, you get on to the plumber. You don't get on to the plumber's wife and moan about what he's done, do you? Well they do with clergy. She's been used as an avenue to get at me . . . Like most clergy wives, she's a very tough person, and she's always been content to make me available, but there's no doubt she's suffered.'

For Anne, it was particularly hurtful being held at arm's length, because when her husband was ordained as an NSM, they stayed on in their own parish, where they had been long-standing members of the Church. 'It was very hard moving almost overnight from being the wife of a lay person to being the wife of an NSM,' she says. 'Friends suddenly became wary, and some stopped inviting us to more risqué parties. We were conscious of people keeping us at a distance because they were unsure of Stephen's new status. It was all very hurtful. Contacts outside the parish remain a lifeline for us.'

Confidentiality can be a barrier to friendship within the parish. There are two sides to the problem: the burden of being privy to the personal problems of other people, and the weight of having no one to share private

116

or parish-related concerns or frustrations with apart from each other.

'Confidentiality is a nuisance,' Clare told me. 'Sometimes it's hard to remember whether something someone told you was in confidence or not, and when other people ask questions about members of the congregation, it can get tricky.' 'It's knowing certain things about people, and not showing that you do, or being in a group and not being able to mention the particular hurt or problem someone is experiencing, even in a helpful way,' says Diana. Liz agrees: 'There are some things we know about people – such as their marriage difficulties – which then make it hard when you see them in a social setting.'

Loyalty can also become an issue. 'I have to be very careful,' says Christine. 'People tend to be very critical of one of my husband's colleagues, and it is hard to remain neutral and not agree.' From my own experience, there was a woman in one parish who regularly used to ask me questions about members of the congregation and the clergy team, which I could not possibly answer. She was a kind and loyal member of the Church and I think it was a combination of her natural interest in other people and a desire to feel involved, and although I was aware that she might feel hurt at being held at a distance, I frequently had to deflect her.

'I'm quick to share and exchange with folk. I'm having to learn to withhold myself from them. I never wanted to do that,' Katie told me sadly. 'We are very guarded, and I think will have to remain so,' says Carol. Joanne finds that confidentiality causes communication problems in her marriage. 'Edward takes it to ridiculous extremes,' she says. 'People have told him things, assuming he would tell me, and when he hasn't, it's led to all manner of misunderstandings.'

Many others, however, claimed that confidentiality caused them no difficulty. 'I had to sign the Official Secrets Act when I started my first job, so it has never been a problem,' says Sheila. 'If you are told something confidential, that is how it must be. Just occasionally, if you want to confide in someone else, it can make you feel isolated.' 'Jonathan doesn't tell me everything and I don't tell him everything,' says Fiona firmly. Sandra agrees: 'Andy and I keep matters absolutely confidential from one another, as we see appropriate. But it is a burden and I am in the process of trying to find someone with whom I personally can "debrief".'

FRIENDSHIP

According to the traditional school of thought, clergy and their families cannot – or should not – have friends within their congregation. While few families would expect their social life to revolve solely round one partner's working life, clergy families none the less usually live, worship, and often go to school, within the parish. I myself would be very sad not to have any friends within my church or village; for me, it goes against the grain of what being part of a community means, and it would be deeply lonely. As far as I am concerned, friendship is an essential part of life. Yet I am also aware that there can be pitfalls.

'I know that the making of close friends within the congregation is sometimes frowned upon, but I could not survive without a small circle of good friends,' Ruth told me. 'As well as helping me through some difficult times, these Church friends have formed a large part of my social life here.' 'I'm pretty gregarious, but the vicar's wife position is a lonely place at times,' says Melanie. 'I like a lot of people in the congregations enormously, but in the past, I have made friends too quickly and then, after six months or so, found that I hadn't got too much in common with them. So I've tried not to be particularly friends with any one person.'

Many people pointed to the importance of being

aware of creating jealousy. 'We have to be cautious,' Tim, a vicar, told me. 'I'm very careful about friendships. It's not that you won't make them, and I do make a point of supporting those with responsibilities in the Church, but I try not to have favourites.'

'I'm slightly uneasy about becoming too close to one person in a congregation, as this becomes cliquey and exclusive,' says Carol. Linda agrees. 'Tensions are sometimes caused by people minding that you have chosen someone else as a friend rather than them. I think this is why we have often been told by older clergy couples that you can't have friends in the parish.' Yet this constraint – in many ways unnatural – can be difficult, especially for the rest of the family, who need friendship as much as anyone else.

Several people said they were aware of hindrances to forming close relationships. 'There is usually someone to be reasonably close to,' says Susan, 'but there are always constraints.' 'I have to admit that now Barbara is ordained, I feel there are some things I can't share with people at church,' says Bill, a clergy husband. 'I'm not a very lonely type, but I have missed good friends to really relax with,' says Janet. 'It's hard to make good friends in this parish, because it is not a mobile population. People here don't really need new friends, because their school friends, grannies, mums and dads all live across the road or round the corner. So it's difficult for an outsider to get beyond a certain point.'

'People in the congregation have always been quite pleasant, but it's not the same as my real friends, who I can have fun with and be more vulnerable with,' says Melanie. 'We can make friends to a certain point, but no further,' agrees Caroline. One or two people commented on the other extreme: avoiding being 'taken over' by people keen to appropriate them. 'It can be a problem keeping people at arm's length, so that they don't swamp me completely,' says Beth. 'Generally, I have lots of

119

friends on all different levels,' says Becky. 'But when we were first married, I had a very possessive woman who tried to "own" me. She then got upset because I refused to be exclusive, and made my life very difficult.'

Several people pointed to the difficulties of making time for friendships. 'Friendships with other couples have been possible, but pressures of time mean that we don't socialize as much as we would like,' says Jo. My own fear is that it is all too easy to lose the habit, and even the ability, to build real friendships. I know several older, workaholic clergy and their wives who, though apparently well-liked and respected, have no actual friends, either in the parish, or beyond, and it is all too easy to see how the situation has arisen. The negative result is not only isolation, but an inevitable narrow-mindedness as it becomes increasingly hard to see beyond the horizons of the parish.

A number of people said their social circles extended well beyond the Church. In each of the two parishes where my husband was a curate, I was extremely fortunate in having women friends who were Roman Catholics, and one aspect of those friendships I particularly valued was the fact that we shared a faith, and yet not the same church. I could let off steam with them in a way I could not with anyone else. Now we live in a village, where we are just as likely to socialize with non-churchgoers as church regulars.

'Our circle of acquaintances is not restricted to our seven congregations,' says Felicity. 'We spend time socially with people involved and uninvolved with the Church.' 'Young children are a great bridge,' says Wendy. 'I have been able to make friends with other mums at the school gates. Some of them happen to be members of the congregation too.' 'I have some good friends in the parish who aren't Christians who treat me just like another friend', says Charlotte.

My own experience is that friendship is vital to

everyone's life, and it is worth going to considerable lengths to nurture old friendships and to cultivate new ones, even when it would be easier not to. As Rhiannon told me, 'There are occasional bad moments in parish ministry. And then I visit a friend or chat it over. I find close friends, honesty and humour *essential* in the ministry.'

WHEN THINGS GO WRONG

Like any other family, clergy families can sometimes find themselves with serious problems. In their study of clergy marriage, Kirk and Leary found that while the divorce rate among the clergy is well below the national average of one in three, this does not mean that they experience fewer marital difficulties. Evidence suggests that, whereas in past years many clergy and their wives struggled grimly on in miserable marriages, in the last decade or two there have been many more cases of legal separation and divorce. This fact has gradually been taken on board by the institutional Church, resulting in the establishment of various measures to be taken in the event of marital breakdown, and debates in recent years in the General Synod on clergy marriage, and, subsequently, the related issue of clergy discipline.

In 1991, the Church of England's Board for Social Responsibility published a paper by Roger Hennessey, a counsellor from the diocese of Norwich, on the breakdown of clergy marriages. His research showed that the factors reported as problems in the marriages were not specific to the clergy: they included adultery, homosexuality, alcoholism and 'workaholism'. Yet, as Kirk and Leary concluded in *Holy Matrimony?*, 'It is the total package of the factors acting in synergy that differentiates clergy marriages from those of the rest of the marrying classes. Taken by itself, each particular pressure may not differ greatly from those experienced by the people of which the clergyman has the care, but there are fewer

121

material compensations for the stress, or protections against it. Furthermore, the internal and external pressures to be a role model for the community, to provide stability in a changing world, to be perfect so that others may bear their imperfections (and this can result in an unwillingness to acknowledge the need for help or to seek it because of the "position" that must be kept up) make clergy marriages unique.'

Meanwhile, in 1997 Dr Lesley MacDonald, an academic from the University of Edinburgh, published the results of a two-year research study of cases of domestic violence within clergy marriages. Her study, which featured in a BBC1 *Here and Now* programme, included graphic accounts of appalling abuse suffered by 23 women, which in some cases had lasted for years. At the time of the programme, Dr MacDonald said that she was in touch with many more clergy wives in similar situations, who had declined to take part in her study, because they were still in the abusive relationship. 'It is particularly hard to accept that people who are very plausible, charismatic and gifted in their professional lives are abusive in their private lives,' she said. 'But this is something that happens in all sectors of society.' Many women had stayed with their husbands because they were frightened no one would believe them, because they did not know where to go for help, or because they felt it was their duty to submit to the violence, because their husband was a 'man of God'.

Whatever the problem (and domestic violence is just one, extreme example), research suggests that clergy and their spouses are very reluctant to seek professional help when they run into marital difficulties. This may be because they simply do not know where to turn for appropriate support, because the clergy are afraid that admitting domestic problems to their archdeacon or bishop might jeopardize their career. The fact that the bishop holds both pastoral and management roles here can be a double bind. Equally, they may find it extraordinarily difficult to admit their 'failure', when they have, however unfairly, been put on a pedestal within the community. Thus, for 'the good of the Church', marital difficulties can be repressed, as a guilty secret, which is counter-productive within the marriage, and makes the shock if the couple eventually separates even greater.

When a clergy marriage finally founders, the family suffers all the usual traumatic effects experienced when any couple split up, combined with the full force of the shock-waves generated throughout the local community and, especially if there is a third party involved, interest from the press. Historically, many wives have found themselves in the daunting position of losing not only their husband, but their home, their income and their position in the community as well. Today, as growing numbers of clergy wives are in employment, they, like most clergy husbands, are at least more likely to have some means of financial support.

A report by the House of Bishops in 1985 recognized that the Church had a certain responsibility ('stemming from the special nature of the clergyman's calling and the way of life of himself and his family') to help pick up some of the pieces in the event of the breakdown of a clergy marriage. In response, a scheme was established whereby every diocese has at least one diocesan visitor, appointed by the Bishop, to lend the spouse (wife, originally) practical help. According to the guidelines for 1996, the job description of the visitor is that they offer non-judgmental support to the deserted spouse at the time of the breakdown, and for as long as necessary while they rebuild their life. Most of the task centres on practical concerns, such as financial, legal and housing matters (with which the diocese will usually assist), and referral to appropriate charities (such as the Corporation of the Sons of the Clergy and the Friends of the Clergy Corporation) or counselling agencies as appropriate.

Meanwhile, Broken Rites – an association of divorced and separated clergy wives – offers support in both the early stages of a break-up, alongside the diocesan visitor, and afterwards on a more long-term basis. According to Christine McMullen, the organization's secretary, there were about 200 members of Broken Rites in 1997, although she describes this as 'the tip of the iceberg'. Members around the country offer support on a regional basis, by telephone, meetings or local support groups.

Not all problems are as acute as marriage breakdown, of course, but most families come under pressure at times; and as we saw in earlier chapters, the majority of spouses believe that there are stresses unique to clergy households. As Kirk and Leary found in their study, 'A job which is often seven days a week, lack of leisure time and holidays, constant nagging worries about money, frequent moves, the inescapability of living "over the shop", the pressures of bearing so many expectations, so much pain, the new skills to be learned, the new role to be discerned, the upheaval and change in the Church, the feeling of being at worst a failure, at best an irrelevance – these factors can take a huge toll on the physical, mental, emotional and spiritual health of the clergy household.' Not only did they find a high level of stress among the clergy in their sample, but an alarmingly high incidence of illness and depression, not merely in the clergy, but also their spouses.

Many of the spouses in my own survey had stories to tell of especially stressful episodes in the course of their partner's ministry, where the pressures inevitably spilled over to affect the rest of the household. This was caused variously by the clergy partner overworking, exhaustion, family difficulties, problematical relationships with the congregation, or the burden of guilt and duty imposed on a spouse becoming too much to bear. 'You know what it's like,' says Caroline. 'The vicar gets to go on any number of retreats or whatever, because he needs a break, but what about us?'

124

'There have been many, many times when it has all got too much,' says Alice. 'There have been times when I've felt as if I was bringing up our family on my own. When our second child was two weeks old, we had to give in to the pressure to have the prayer group and coffee morning in our home. It was such a struggle with a newborn and a two-year-old to keep the house presentable and keep my sanity. William was just not around to give me any extra help. I felt as if I was on a roundabout going too fast, which would not stop. I did not want the intrusion into my home, but the circumstances we were in, in that particular parish, meant that things could only be changed slowly, and changing those regular meetings in our house was by no means at the top of the list. I don't know how I coped, probably by shouting at my husband a lot, and having long telephone conversations with my mother. I can remember sitting in the prayer group holding the baby and feeling as if I hated everyone there – not the ideal feelings to take to the group. I felt they were making my life miserable, but I had to try to appear as if I was coping – a vicious circle. The difference in our life since we left that parish is unbelievable.'

'It all gets too much, usually about once every year,' says Harriet, who is very actively involved in her husband's ministry. 'Just after Christmas is a particularly vulnerable time. I find I've got too busy, trying to fit too many things into each day over an extended period, with the result that I become exhausted. Typically, I get upset over something that is the last straw, spend a day in tears, and then realize I am exhausted. Then I make a list of what has to go, and what I feel God is really calling me to do. After a couple of days I bounce back and am ready to go again.'

'Sometimes I've been too involved in the politics of church life, and absorbed some of the criticisms of others personally,' says Mary. 'I've coped by removing myself into a job situation, and worked out coping strategies for dealing with "whingers".' 'Things are bad when he gets stressed, and throws wobblies. I bear the brunt,' Carol told me. Felicity supports this. 'The workload and demands tend to build up, and I become fearful for Sam's health and disappointed in the quality of our time together. I have wept, prayed and got angry.' 'What we need right now is some time off,' says Jo, 'but fitting holiday around what's going on in the church is very difficult.'

Others reported that it was only when they reached breaking point that other church members had realized the strain they were under. 'On one occasion, Stephen was being criticized for something out of his control,' remembers Anne. 'I actually burst into floods of tears. The person concerned was so amazed that she has been very supportive since.' 'There have been many times when I've resented the job that takes over our lives, although I suppose it has never become too much to cope with,' says Wendy. 'The worst time was after an arson attack on the church and hall, and my husband was completely absorbed with raising money and getting materials donated for a new hall. He was on the phone all day, talked about it at every mealtime, dreamt about it, and became emotionally and mentally exhausted. I remember I broke down in tears when talking to the churchwarden and his wife. I think that people realizing how hard he was working did help a little. The support of friendship was there but we just had to wait until the hall was finished for things to get better.'

FINDING SUPPORT

'I once mentioned that I was going on a clergy wives conference,' Melanie told me. '"Don't feel you have to" was one response; "Learning to make cucumber sandwiches?" another. Both were PCC members – one person not thinking I might need support, and the other so flippant. So many clergy wives I've met are lonely in their marriages – restricted in being able to follow their own interests by their husband's job and unsupported by diocesan structures, because the wide variety in church-manship makes fellowship very threatening. Coffee evenings have been the extent of the deanery support I've been offered. And such support structures as there are tend to be run by the people who have needed them most: the loneliest, least able to make friends for themselves. They've been pretty ghastly.'

It can be just as hard for the clergy and their spouses to acknowledge their need for support as it is for the congregation to recognize the way the pressures on a clergy household build up. Yet, as in any family, recog-nizing signs of strain before serious damage is done is essential to relationships functioning healthily. Christine McMullen of Broken Rites told me that, in her opinion, marriage support for clergy and their spouses would be far more effective than any marriage preparation could be. She pointed out that the General Synod report on clergy discipline, *Under Authority*, published in 1996, covered some of the concerns addressed by Broken Rites – the need for proper support, accountability and super-vision for the clergy – which she says could be both releasing and empowering for clergy and their families.

But how do you provide useful support for clergy spouses – such a broad group of people, all of whom will have very different needs? As one of the clergy in *Revelations* observed, 'Wives are in a cleft stick in all of this. My wife gets invitations to various clergy meetings, but she doesn't want to meet clergy wives because she only ends up either being totally overwhelmed by the super-efficient, wonderful, all-singing, all-dancing unpaid curates who involve themselves in the work left, right and centre or she gets to hear all the same moans that she's got, with no resolution.'

Many of the people who took part in my survey

expressed reservations about meeting together with other clergy spouses. 'I think a good support network might be helpful, but clergy spouses are all so different,' Sue told me. 'We don't necessarily have a lot in common. Some older clergy wives are a bit threatened by the non-traditional ones, and I end up feeling a bit judged, or that I have to justify my approach.' 'The only clergy wives events I've ever been invited to have been very tedious,' says Marion. 'There's this idea that if you just bring the wives together, that in itself equals support. But we don't always get on, and the subject matter at meetings might be something quite obscure, like liturgical dance. And when do you meet? If you're working, the day-time is no good, and evenings or weekends are always difficult to arrange.'

A bishop's wife I spoke to on this subject was clear that spouses should be supported in whatever role they wished to play. 'We need to support people in their choices, without reinforcing the stereotypes,' she said. 'Recently, I was talking to some of the spouses in this diocese about what they would like to see on offer, and one wife said to me, "I'm not interested in quiet days, but if you're talking about noisy nights, then count me in." Others do want the quiet days and, of course, they need the opportunity for that too.'

In the Anglican Church in the United States, ECUSA, a number of formal networks of support for clergy and their families do exist. In 1986, an organization called the Episcopal Family Network set up a research and action programme called the Clergy Family Project, with the stated aim of 'strengthening the lives of clergy and those in relationships with them, and promote their well-being'. The Project acts as a consultancy to dioceses, assessing the needs of the clergy and their families, and assisting the dioceses in the development of appropriate organizations, resources and policies to support them. Dioceses also have their own clergy family support ministry, to assist bishops in the provision of pastoral care to clergy households.

As my American friend put it when she wrote to me, 'There has long been a greater receptivity here than in Britain to the insights of psychology. The Church here understands that when clergy are not well cared for, they cannot be expected to care well for others. It recognizes that caring for clergy means caring for their families, and that this entails everything from adequate salaries and accommodation to consideration for the needs and preferences of clergy wives. From my experience, the Church of England seems to think that this approach is unnecessarily indulgent and that the priest and his family should gladly suffer an array of deprivations, and that their parishes will be none the worse for it.'

In this country, a number of spouses told me they had no idea where to turn for confidential and appropriate help within the structure of the Church. 'I don't think the Church is very good at a personnel level,' says Jim, a clergy husband. 'It's not very supportive. I'm not aware of anywhere I could go for professional help if I needed it. You have to fend for yourself.' 'Our marriage is under strain at the moment,' says Katie. 'I need support from the Church right now, but I don't know where that confidential help is.'

Some dioceses do provide handbooks specifically for clergy spouses, of varying degrees of usefulness. One diocesan visitor told me that a number of dioceses are reluctant to publish the details of their own visitors, 'because they don't want to advertise the fact that clergy marriages break down', which, as she points out, is rather like not telling anyone the 999 number, in case you frighten them. In my own diocese, while the general diocesan handbook does include the names and addresses of diocesan visitors, there are no details about counsellors. Instead, I am referred to my husband's Archdeacon or Bishop, who will provide a list, although in the event of a serious problem I have to say this would be the last avenue I would actually want to pursue. Other dioceses, I know, more usefully publish a list of phone numbers and special areas of expertise of counsellors who deal with a whole range of problems, so that clergy and/ or spouses can refer themselves directly to a specialist, without having to make any contact with officialdom.

One source of support for clergy and their families is the Society of Martha and Mary, a charity based in Devon that offers support, counselling and residential facilities for clergy and their families. 'We exist because ministry is a demanding vocation, very fulfilling, but at times draining and isolated,' says the Society's publicity. 'When a crisis strikes it is important to have good-quality, accessible, affordable care available. Equally important, but so often overlooked, is the need to take preventive care when things are going well. Allowing time for adequate rest, reflection and renewal, as well as the stimulus of meeting new people and learning new skills, are all necessary.' With this in mind, they offer regular '12,000-mile services', and a range of other pastoral programmes. Confidentiality is taken very seriously: 'It is distressing how many people who come to Mary and Martha have tried to share work, personal or marital difficulties with their line managers within the Church, only to find their story circulating on the gossip grapevine,' says the booklet. 'Basic rules are that no one is "sent" here, and we report back to no one within family or Church structures unless our guests specifically request this. Professional support and supervision of team members provides independent accountability and a safeguard for guest welfare. Confidentiality is of paramount importance at all times.'

On a less formal level, some of the spouses I spoke to had their own support systems. 'I have a whole network of friends, through my job, and they are nothing to do with the parish or the Church, fortunately,' Linda told me. Others turn to family or friends from past lives for support. 'My mother is my lifeline,' says Lucy. 'Being another clergy wife, she understands what it is like.' Sally, whose husband is a curate, told me that the spouses group from theological college had grown into a loose association of women who kept in touch after the move into parishes. 'But people's experiences differ so much, I don't know if I could prescribe appropriate support for anyone else', she says. Wendy commented on the difference moving back to their home town had made. 'Two years ago, after Peter's curacy, we moved back here, where most of our family still live. They have been a huge support to us,' she says. 'Living in an area where people live close to their families, it's been great to feel normal, to go for coffee with my Mum, or for my Dad to pick up the children from school occasionally, and for us to see our brothers and sisters-in-law socially. It has helped us to escape the parish and to talk about normal things.'

Perhaps the strongest message to come through is that the support structures need to be well and truly in place before a minor problem turns into a crisis. This is because adequate and ongoing back-up can be the best preventive measure and if a serious difficulty does emerge, there is a tried and tested source of help. While some clergy families would point to the enormous warmth and friendship they meet within their congregations, there are circumstances where support outside the parish is absolutely essential. And it is just as important for spouses to have a listening ear as it is for the priest. Whether this involves finding support on a deanery or diocesan level, regular visits to a spiritual director, taking up an interest or job that removes you from the immediate confines of the parish or just spending time with friends, it has to be worth investing time in developing a network of solid friendships, both for pleasure and enjoyment, and also so that the foundations of sound support are in place when help is most needed.

8

CHANGING PATTERNS
OF MINISTRY

In the past 30 years or so, we have witnessed considerable social upheaval in Britain. Major changes have occurred in the ways we think about work, gender relations, family life and theology – the consequences of which are all far-reaching. These changes have been echoed – albeit often after a time-lag – within the Church.

The shape of the ordained ministry has changed, too. The Church of England has faced major financial difficulties, and there has been a gradual but damaging decline in the numbers of clergy, with the result that parishes are being grouped together, and priests are spread ever more thinly over increasingly wider geographical areas. Meanwhile, after decades of debate in the Church of England, the first women were eventually ordained to the diaconate in 1987, and then in 1994 to the priesthood. At the same time, non-stipendiary and local non-stipendiary ministry schemes have been developed with varying degrees of enthusiasm by different dioceses.

All of these changes have resulted in a rethinking of the role of the ordained ministry, and have had knock-on effects for clergy households. What, for example, do parishes make of clergy husbands? Is a clergywoman who happens to be married to a clergyman also assumed to be a clergy wife? Do clergy wives feel threatened – or heartened – by the arrival of ordained women? How do churchgoers and clergy respond to increasing lay leadership?

MINISTRY AND CHANGE

The vicar's daughter is getting married. The vicar greets the bride and her father at the church door and leads them up the aisle. How?

For many people, it is still hard to adjust to the fact that we have female priests in the Church of England. Although many objectors to the ordination of women may have deeply held convictions, anecdotal evidence suggests that people often find the idea of the ordination of women harder to accept than the fact, as in parish after parish women priests are quietly getting on with the job, their ministry welcomed and valued. The implications for clergy families in general, however, are hard to tease out. It is still too early to make any useful generalizations about whether or not clergy households in which the priest happens to be female are any different from those where the priest is male. Although women have been deaconesses and deacons for many more years than they have been priests, it is their ordination to the priesthood (still very recent history) which has opened the way to posts of sole responsibility, with all the baggage that comes with them.

The ordination of women to the priesthood is not the only change. It has long been observed that one aspect of the social change of post-war Britain has been the increasing marginalization of the Church. The clergy no longer hold the central position in the social and cultural life of the nation they once did, and the truths they proclaim are increasingly considered by the greater proportion of the public to be irrelevant to everyday life.

Meanwhile, the economic problems faced by the

133

Church have led to a revision of the strategies for the deployment of clergy, and a new emphasis on both non-stipendiary ordained ministry and lay leadership. For some members of the Church – both clergy and lay – such change is very threatening. Some clergy worry for their future job prospects, and there is a more general-ized fear in some quarters that when the traditions of the Church are overturned, the Church itself is under threat.

NEW CLERGY HOUSEHOLDS

The first man I spoke to about his role as a clergy husband simply did not understand what I was talking about. 'What do you mean, my role?' he asked. 'What sort of role?' Did he, I asked, take any active part in his wife's church, and had he come across any expectations that he should be involved in the parish? 'Well,' he conceded, obviously still a little at sea, 'I do usually go to church, if that's what you mean.'

I don't know whether to be heartened at this man's complete freedom to be himself or annoyed on behalf of all the generations of women for whom, by simple virtue of their sex, the same query would have elicited an instant (and weary) comprehension of its meaning. Of all the clergy spouses I spoke to, I have yet to come across a husband for whom expectations or identity were real issues. The baggage (flower-arranging, Mothers Union, sensible shoes) just doesn't seem to travel across the gender gap. Of much greater concern to the husbands I spoke to was the question of negotiating family time in the context of a job that has unpredictable and often antisocial hours – a concern shared, of course, by any number of families in secular work.

True 'clergy husbands' are still relatively thin on the ground in Britain. As women have only been priests since 1994, the number of female incumbents is still extremely small at the moment. The number of women

134

who have been ordained is only a fraction of the number of men, anyway, and more clergywomen are currently single than married. Many of those who are married also have priests for husbands. Thus, the relatively small number of unordained men who are married to women priests remain something of a novelty.

In June 1996, *The Sunday Times* carried a piece about one vicar's husband, who (according to the article, anyway) appeared to have done as much as he could to turn himself into a 'vicar's wife', in spite of his own obvious prejudices (he describes attending a clergy wives' social evening, 'the only man among 70 or 80 mostly middle-aged women', and asks, 'What was a 46-year-old consultant engineer – who had just done a hard day's work in a distinctly macho environment – doing sipping sweet sherry with the matrons of the diocese amid talk of jumble sales and flower arranging?'). He wrote that he had had to create his own role as a clergy husband, there being no role models around. In spite of that macho job of his, he had styled himself as chief maker of tea ('I carry the trays round here') and telephone answerer ('The phone never stops ringing at home, and I try to field the calls and protect [her] when she is tired or busy'). While he draws the line at flower arranging, he mows the churchyard grass and moves pianos when required. The locals, he says, don't know quite what to make of him.

Another interesting role reversal emerges in the experience of Alistair, who gave up his own job as an industrial chemist to care for the children full-time while his wife continued in her ministry. They felt that his pattern of shift-work, combined with his wife's uncertain hours, put too much pressure on the family. Now the three children are at school, he is looking for part-time work that might fit round the needs of the family. When they lived in a UPA parish, he was active in the parish. 'I was very involved in community work there,' he says. 'But it was mainly doing "male" things, such as the accounts. Now we are in the country, and Shirley has seven churches, I am less involved because there is the tradition that the Rector does everything.' He has met none of 'the standard clergy wife expectations', he says. 'We've only been here 18 months, but the only thing that has come up was the flowers for harvest festival. In the past, the Rector's wife has always done them. The parish assumed I wouldn't want to, so then they thought they should ask my wife.'

Churchgoers do not seem to have the same perceptions of clergy husbands that they are so often reported – still – to have of wives. 'When we moved into this parish, I'm quite sure the question to a female spouse would have been "What are you planning to do?"' says Bill. 'But no one ever asked me that. Instead, the question was always, "How do you earn your living?" Having said that, I believe they are pleased I am so involved in church.' 'I don't perceive any expectations,' says Chris. 'I think I'm saved from all that. It's Annie's job, not mine. If I go to church, I am there as me. But I don't really get involved. For instance, my hobby is rifle shooting, and sometimes I go off on a Sunday morning and do this instead of going to church. I don't know if people find this unacceptable, but it's what I enjoy doing. I haven't had any adverse comments.'

James, a professional musician and church organist, says he thinks he would be more involved in church life were he not married to the vicar. 'For instance, one of the churchwardens is standing down and we've talked about me taking that on. In normal circumstances, I probably would,' he says. 'But I am very aware that with a small electoral roll, we could very easily get a stranglehold on the church. Generally I try not to get involved too much. That way, I think I'm more use to Jenny as a sounding board.'

Jim agrees. 'I do avoid getting too tied up with positions on the PCC,' he says. 'I think as a clergy spouse you should take a back seat or you become too involved as a family. But I do a lot of the kiddies' work – I run the Sunday school and a holiday club. Both congregations have been very accepting of me. The one place I have met an odd reaction is the social club on our estate, where I drop in for a drink sometimes. They've certainly treated me very warily.

'I think the most difficult thing I've found since Rosie's ordination is the amount of time she has to work, and the number of evenings she is out. That's been difficult to cope with. We have 4 children, aged between 11 and 17, and keeping track of them all is hard enough. At least, being a teacher, I can be around after school and in the holidays. But the demands – emotional and physical – on Rosie do affect me. Sometimes I feel there is not enough left at the end of the day for me. That's been really difficult.'

The ordination of women means that there is now also a growing number of couples where both partners are ordained. While for many clergywomen – particularly those who have been ordained after a long wait – their ordination and the fulfilment of their ministry is a cause of great joy, a number I spoke to were frustrated by the difficulties of working out two ordained ministries in one marriage. There are some dioceses, for example, where a woman is only ever ordained to non-stipendiary ministry if her husband is already a priest. Even where this is not the case, there are the problems of finding two parish jobs near enough each other or a job in a sector ministry for one partner.

'It's fine at the moment,' says Megan, currently taking a career break to look after her young children. 'The bishop made it quite clear at Steve's licensing that the parish was not getting two for the price of one. No one's descended on me to do things, and I'm quite happy with that, although I do find it odd after my curacy, suddenly not knowing who all the people at church are. But I have to face reality: to find the type of job I really want in the future will be very difficult. I don't like the thought of farming out the children on Sunday mornings. There aren't enough sector jobs to go around, and parish ministry is going to be a big problem if we both want to get paid.'

Jill, who has worked part-time in the same parish as her husband since the birth of her first child, says that she finds it difficult to know which hat she is wearing. 'I said to Pete only this week, "I don't know if I am doing this as me or as your wife or because it is work." People have been great – they have been falling over backwards not to overload me, but then that sometimes means they don't ask me to do something, like making a casserole or whatever, that they would have asked another mother with a part-time job, which I feel I could have done.'

Amy, also a mother of young children, says she is delighted to be able to do some of the work in the parish her husband wouldn't otherwise manage to do. 'I'm not officially working at all, but I can get on with all sorts of things that I know Robert will never get round to. That's satisfying professionally for me. It's been lovely in the parish as well, because I think they felt quite threatened by the thought of me coming in as a woman priest, but the sorts of things I do could be done by anyone, really.'

CHANGING THE RULES

The goalposts have moved. The make-up of churches, of styles of Church leadership and of clergy households has become increasingly diverse over the last couple of decades, and such change shows every sign of continuing. That there are implications for clergy families, both positive and negative, seems unavoidable. For example, wives of clergymen are faced with the fact that their husbands may now for the first time have female colleagues, with whom they work closely and intensely. Some women may feel very threatened by this – sexually and, if they happen to have a very active role within the

138

parish, emotionally, in that they may fear their own contribution to Church life might no longer be needed. Some of the most vehement opponents of women's ordination appear to be women who, had they only been born a generation later, might very well have been at the front of the queue outside their bishop's door.

In this context, it is interesting to consider the case of ECUSA. In the United States, women have been ordained for considerably longer than their British counterparts, and are fully integrated into the Church. According to my correspondent there, who has been a clergy wife in both the Church of England and ECUSA, the ordination of women to the priesthood has changed things for the better for clergy wives. 'In North America there is greater sensitivity in society as a whole to the concerns of women, and this is mirrored in the Church,' she says. 'Most of the clergy wives whom I know in this country have professional careers, whereas most of those I knew in England did not. The Episcopal Church has therefore been compelled to adjust more rapidly to the idea of autonomous clergy wives. The longer experience in ECUSA of both female priests and their husbands has done much to undermine the conventional role of the clergy wife, which has been decidedly beneficial.

'Lay ministry is also more advanced in ECUSA. In most Episcopal churches, there is literally no need for the priest's wife to take on parochial duties, as there are ample (and well-trained) lay people to perform them. In fact, so much pride is taken by lay people in their contribution to the parish that a clergy wife who assumes too much responsibility is frowned upon. I have heard Episcopalians make such remarks about overly active clergy wives as, "This church does not need a 'rectorine'," and "This parish has a father, it doesn't need a mother." It has been my experience that in ECUSA a clergy wife is far more likely to be criticized for too much rather than not enough involvement in parish life.'

Although there is no guarantee that the North American experience will automatically apply to the Church of England, it seems that such patterns are already beginning to emerge here. It is apparent that clergy husbands are not perceived simply to be substitute clergy wives: a female vicar may bring a very different approach to the job to her male counterpart, and the notions of wifehood and husbandhood are not so easily transposed. As the old ways of doing things gradually break down, so the spin-offs for the rest of the household will change accordingly.

Change can appear very threatening, of course, but it can be very liberating. There is clearly more work to be done on the links between spirituality and sexuality, the different qualities male and female clergy might bring to the ministry and the dynamics of clergy families. If women clergy are, by virtue of their sex, assumed by parishes to have a stronger duty of care to their families than their male counterparts, then perhaps this attitude will eventually filter down to benefit all clergy households. Meanwhile, the full development of collaborative, 'every person' ministry is clearly an essential element in the future of the Church, a context in which of course the 'traditional' clergy spouse will be more than welcome as an active lay person. How we respond to the challenge of change, both within the Church and within our households, says a lot about the health of the relationships on which both are founded.

9

WHERE DOES THIS
LEAVE US?

It was always likely that the descriptions of life in clergy households would vary widely from one couple or family, parish or church to another. We all have our own individual strengths and weaknesses, and our particular struggles and bugbears; and we have all come to our current positions by different paths. What, though, has changed for the clergy in the last 20 or 30 years? And how has this changed the way today's clergy households are fashioned?

A fundamental factor contributing to the differences between the clergy households of today and those of 30 years ago has been the social upheaval of recent decades. The revolution in attitudes brought about by the women's movement (almost old hat in the secular world) has gradually filtered down into the Church, into our models of marriage, ministry, gender relations. This is most obvious in the ordination of women, although there remain considerable pockets of the Church in which women in ministry still face inequality and discrimination. The growing acceptance of the fundamental equality of men and women has meanwhile had a considerable impact on our ideas about what might constitute Christian marriage. Furthermore, it is now far more common for a clergy wife to be in paid employment – after the earliest years of any child-rearing have passed – than to be at home and helping in the parish full-time.

As Sally, a solicitor, and both the daughter and wife of clergymen, says, 'It's accepted that I work. It wasn't for my mother. Similarly, there is little expectation on me to give up my free time, while she was always obliged to run groups and bake cakes. I'm sure it's part of a general move towards the acceptance of women's increasing autonomy.'

Alice, also a clergy daughter and now a clergy wife in her twenties, agrees. 'I think clergy wives have learnt to discover their own role, and stick to it despite external pressures. All the clergy wives I know of my own age go out to work. I think this is an excellent shield against pressures from the parish. By distancing ourselves from the parish we avoid many confrontations with those who have ideas about what their vicar's wife should do. For myself, having made the decision to stay at home and bring up our children, I have at times found it difficult not to do what those around me expect me to do without seeming rude. The easiest thing so often is to comply. You have to be firm about what you want and not let yourself be bullied.'

Meanwhile, there are also many more couples in secular jobs facing the challenge of juggling two jobs, family life, faith and other interests. Couples now enter marriage and family life with different sets of expectations than they did just a generation ago. The pressures of modern-day living are immense, we are told; but at least some of these pressures, such as the importance of nurturing family relationships, are more commonly acknowledged. Christians can contribute to the current debate on the future of the family by making positive choices about working sensible hours and investing time in each other.

Ministry, meanwhile, has also changed. There continues to be a gradual, if very slow, shift away from the old pattern of the male priest, perceived as solely in charge and spiritually superior to a dependent passive flock, towards a celebration of a more collaborative style of ministry, encompassing non-stipendiary ministry and greater lay leadership, as well as, of course, the full participation of women priests. Churchgoers are having to adapt to different styles of ministry and change their expectations of the clergy and their partners.

'The expectations of vicars' wives have definitely changed,' says Vanessa, a clergy wife of some years' standing. 'It's much less rigid now, particularly as more women are working outside the home and simply cannot do all that clergy wives have traditionally done. I suspect and hope that as more women enter the ministry, and as more men take on the status of clergy spouse, fewer assumptions will be made about a vicar's wife, and fewer demands placed upon her.'

'There's much less pressure from the Church these days,' says Emma, whose husband was ordained fairly recently. 'That's largely thanks to those who fought this battle before me.'

Some of the clergy wives who took part in my research were confident that the battle was long since won, although many more testified to still having to meet expectations from the parish. In spite of all the very real changes, elements of the old stereotype persist. At the very least, it seems that there often remains an assumption that a clergy wife will *be* a certain sort of person, behave in a particular way and create a certain sort of family, even if it is not assumed that she will automatically *do* anything in particular in the Church. A number of people said that their experience was that it was not so much members of the congregation who had stereotypical ideas about them, but other members of the community. Overall, the picture is patchy, and the evidence anecdotal, but it appears that the identity is still hanging on in there, especially in rural areas.

'It was made very clear to me when we moved here that there were no expectations of me in the church, which is fine,' says Lucy, a curate's wife. 'But it is still impossible to become an active member of the congregation on your own terms, because whatever you do or say reflects on your spouse or is seen as coming from them rather than from you. You become totally impotent as a Christian. When we move I'll probably go to a different church.'

'Expectations are definitely less formal, less traditional,' says Becky. 'We can work now, without raising eyebrows, and keep our surnames. I genuinely don't see myself as any different to others at church, but I still get introduced as the vicar's wife. Generally, though, I've found it very easy to be myself. This has caused the odd upset, such as when I went on the bouncy castle after having opened the church fête. But the greatest danger is when you try to fit into a mould or try to please people. My theory is no one has a real problem with you if you are genuinely yourself.'

The great majority of spouses feel that there are stresses specific to the clergy lifestyle. Many spouses, however, were just as keen to emphasize the positive aspects of being part of a clergy household. Several said their position gave them a unique and fulfilling role within a church community; a number used the word 'privileged' to describe how they saw their niche.

'It has been a privilege to be involved in ministry with my husband,' says Mary, who is in her fifties. 'Yes, it has created pressures within our home life, but maybe no more than have to be sorted out by any couple at different life stages.' 'I enjoy it, and I feel called to it,' says Rhiannon, a counsellor and mother of four. 'I feel my involvement in Church life is what I would do if I wasn't married to a vicar – I choose to do it. I've learnt over the years to say "No" to things I can't do or don't want to do. I hope clergy wives are freer to be themselves now and use their gifts where they choose, working or non-working.'

'Sometimes I think clergy and their wives can be so weighed down by the difficulties of the life that they forget the benefits,' says Fiona. 'In both churches where we have been, I have felt loved and cared for in a way that any other newcomer would have been glad of. It seems for every plus there is a minus and vice versa.'

'I haven't been a clergy wife for very long,' says Jo. 'But I do think perceptions are changing. Our church and community have been particularly pleased to have a young family in the Rectory, and have been so welcoming.' 'I feel positive when I am feeling strong enough to be confident in the boundaries I have set for myself, which I know are not approved of by a large, mainly female section of our congregation,' says Melanie, a mother of four. 'On bad days, though, I feel thoroughly inadequate. Fortunately, the strong days by far outnumber the bad days!'

'What I don't like is living in a vicarage and subsisting on a clergy stipend, and being expected to play a supporting role in my husband's ministry. I dislike not being an ordinary member of a congregation, and constantly living under the watchful eyes of the parish,' says Catherine. 'But I do appreciate the larger opportunities for friendship and participation in the community I am offered. I enjoy the extent to which my husband and I inhabit the same world of experience and people. And I am grateful for the spiritual resources that have been made available to me through my husband.'

There are, however, certain pressures associated with living in a clergy household, some of which could usefully be addressed. It seems obvious that healthy clergy families will ultimately lead to a stronger Church and, conversely, that if the clergy neglect their own emotional, spiritual and physical needs, this will, in the end, have a damaging effect on both themselves and their ministry.

Care for clergy families is not an optional extra for the Church, it is a necessity.

The subject of selection and training for the ministry, and the appropriate level of involvement for the rest of the family is debated regularly. Several of the spouses who took part in my survey felt overlooked or ignored in the train of events leading up to their partner's ordination. 'When Stephen was considering going forward for ordination, I was asked if his ordination would cause problems in our marriage. I felt the DDO just wanted to tick a box,' says Anne. She believes partners should be properly prepared. 'There should be a course for partners. We all deal with the situation differently, and there is no right way of going about it – there are different ways of being a clergy spouse just as there are different ways of being a priest. But it needs sorting out by the couple, and help should be available.' 'ABM should interview partners as a matter of course,' believes Joanne. 'Their suitability to the lifestyle should be taken into consideration at the time of selection.'

Others strongly object to the idea of 'vetting'. 'I stagger to remember that I was jointly – if not more than – interviewed for theological college,' says Sandra. 'There should be no thought that everyone going to theological college is somehow duty-bound to share a joint vocation, particularly not now that women may be ordained in their own right.'

Others felt that better training for both clergy and their partners was the answer. After all, for ordinands who are already married, their ordination vows will be taken from within the context of their marriage vows, and the need for a couple to work through what this might mean at an early stage might prevent a lot of grief in the future.

Quite what this would mean in practice is less easy to pinpoint. Some spouses felt no amount of training could have helped. 'In a way it's rather like the job itself,' says

Fiona. 'Nothing can really prepare you for it; it's mostly a matter of learning as you go along. But as a clergy wife, I would have appreciated some practical advice – such as specific guidance on how to deal with awkward customers at the door.' 'It's very difficult to be prepared and in one sense I didn't want to face it all beforehand,' says Janet. 'I did go to a curates' wives conference when we were at college, which was good and cemented friendships with like-minded people in similar situations.'

'It is difficult to know what kind of preparation would be helpful, as the needs vary so much from person to person,' says Harriet, who was married for 23 years before her husband was ordained. 'Some of the prospective clergy wives I met at college seemed very poorly equipped emotionally to deal with what lay ahead. Probably courses on knowing yourself and being secure in your relationship with God would be of most benefit, together with experiences shared by clergy wives about how they have coped, so that there is some awareness of the stresses involved.' 'I would have appreciated hearing from people who were already clergy wives as to what life was like, the good bits and bad bits,' agrees Clare. 'What about assertiveness training?' suggests Sally.

There are one or two specific and practical suggestions, none of which are new, but which are still worth reiterating as they may be helpful in avoiding some of the potential difficulties of living in a clergy household. The first is the matter of setting boundaries. Clergy need to make a concerted effort to distinguish between work and home life, and to take responsibility for ensuring that time off is given a high priority. This may require a high degree of self-discipline and organization, but most of all a belief in the importance of spending quality time with the rest of the household. It may also mean being very clear with the congregation, installing an answerphone and rearranging or relocating meetings. All working hours need limits; we are none of us indispensable and genuine crises – when, of course, the clergy want to be available – are relatively few and far between.

Similarly, it is very important for the family to feel that they have their own physical space, on which they have first claim and which will not be invaded for the purposes of work. This will be easier to manage in some clergy houses than in others, and is a relevant factor to consider when viewing the accommodation that goes with any possible new job. Some people may be fortunate in having access to a bolt-hole, in reach of home, where they can escape the telephone and doorbell for uninterrupted time together. If it is remotely possible financially, it is worth having a cottage, camper van, boat or caravan parked in a local farmer's field to go to.

Again, many clergy spouses pointed out the importance of having someone to talk to outside the immediate Church circle, and it is very important to put time and energy into developing a strong network of friendships. This may be through a spouse's job, friendships from theological college, links in the diocese or any other social contact. Similarly, many spouses would find it a huge benefit to find some form of spiritual support, whether with a spiritual director, mentor or prayer partner. The spouse's faith and opportunities for fellowship and growth should not be neglected, either pre-ordination or post-ordination.

It would also be a very positive move if every diocese were able to offer the opportunity for confidential counselling, so that clergy and members of their family had somewhere reliable to turn for help, independent of Church structures, to tackle problems before they get to the point of no return. Sometimes just a 'safe' place in which to work through changes, job moves or working practices within the household as new circumstances arise would be enough. Some families may find that making the change from one lifestyle to another involves considerable adjustment and they need to know where to find useful support.

Meanwhile, when job-hunting, it is worth thinking very carefully about the factors that will affect the whole family, and being clear about what will or will not work, in terms of housing, schooling, a spouse's job prospects, nearness to the wider family or recreational opportunities – whatever happen to be the elements which are particularly important for the happy functioning of the individual family. This is not unreasonable.

This last consideration probably comes under the heading of 'self-awareness'. It is important to be as realistic as possible about both parish and family life, and about how they will fit together. We need to be aware of the issues that are likely to arise and to have common-sense strategies for tackling them. We need to believe in God's pleasure and belief in ourselves, our marriages and our family relationships. We need the confidence to love ourselves as we love our neighbours and to become the people God wants us to be.

REFERENCES AND
FURTHER READING

Archbishops' Commission on Rural Areas, *Faith in the Countryside*, Countryman, 1990.

Archbishops' Commission on Urban Priority Areas, *Faith in the City*, Church House Publishing, 1985.

Archbishops' Commission on Urban Priority Areas, *Staying in the City: Faith in the City 10 years on*, Church House Publishing, 1995.

Shelagh Brown (Ed.), *Married to the Church?*, SPCK, 1983.

Janet Finch, *Married to the Job?*, George Allen and Unwin, 1983.

General Synod, *Under Authority: Report on clergy discipline*, Church House Publishing, 1996.

Robin Greenwood, *Transforming Priesthood*, SPCK, 1994.

Steve Ann Henshall, *Not Always Murder at the Vicarage*, Triangle, 1991.

Ceridwen Higginson, *Such As We Are: A book about the parson's wife, by parsons' wives*, DLT, 1967.

House of Bishops, *Issues in Human Sexuality*, Church House Publishing, 1991.

Mary Kirk and Tom Leary, *Holy Matrimony? An exploration of marriage and ministry*, Lynx, 1994.

Mary Loudon, *Revelations: The clergy questioned*, Hamish Hamilton, 1994.

The Society for Promoting Christian Knowledge (SPCK) has as its purpose three main tasks:

- **Communicating the Christian faith in its rich diversity**

- **Helping people to understand the Christian faith and to develop their personal faith**

- **Equipping Christians for mission and ministry**

SPCK Worldwide serves the Church through Christian literature and communication projects in over 100 countries. Special schemes also provide books for those training for ministry in many parts of the developing world. SPCK Worldwide's ministry involves Churches of many traditions. This worldwide service depends upon the generosity of others and all gifts are spent wholly on ministry programmes, without deductions.

SPCK Bookshops support the life of the Christian community by making available a full range of Christian literature and other resources, and by providing support to bookstalls and book agents throughout the UK. SPCK Bookshops' mail order department meets the needs of overseas customers and those unable to have access to local bookshops.

SPCK Publishing produces Christian books and resources, covering a wide range of inspirational, pastoral, practical and academic subjects. Authors are drawn from many different Christian traditions, and publications aim to meet the needs of a wide variety of readers in the UK and throughout the world.

The Society does not necessarily endorse the individual views contained in its publications, but hopes they stimulate readers to think about and further develop their Christian faith.

For further information about the Society, please write to:
SPCK, Holy Trinity Church, Marylebone Road,
London NW1 4DU, United Kingdom.